Charles Downer Hazen

# THE FRENCH REVOLUTION AND NAPOLEON

 ARCADIA PRESS

# CONTENTS

# THE FRENCH REVOLUTION
# AND NAPOLEON

# PREFACE

No historian believes that history repeats itself. Yet, between different ages there are frequently striking analogies and resemblances. It is problems that repeat themselves, not the conditions which determine their solution. One of these problems, recurrent in European annals, is that of the maintenance of a certain balance of power among the various nations as essential to their freedom, the maintenance of a situation to which they are accustomed and which they have found tolerable, a change in which would be prejudicial or dangerous to their peace and safety. Several times in modern history this balance has been threatened and Europe has purchased immunity from servitude by freely giving its life blood that life might remain and might be worth living.

To an age like our own, caught in the grip of a world war, whose issues, however incalculable, will inevitably be profound, there is much instruction to be gained from the study of a similar crisis in the destinies of humanity a century ago. The most dramatic and most impressive chapter of modern history was written by the French Revolution and by Napoleon. And between that period and our own not only are there points of interesting and suggestive comparison but there is also a distinct line of causation connecting the two.

For the convenience of those who may wish to review this memorable and instructive period I have brought together in this volume the chapters dealing with it in my Modern European History. In the opening twentieth century, as in the opening nineteenth, mankind has been driven to the ordeal by battle by the resolve to preserve the most cherished things of life. Now, as then, civilization hangs upon the arbitrament of the sword. It is not churches alone that owe their existence and their power to the blood of the martyrs. The most precious rights of nations and of individuals have not only been achieved, but have been maintained inviolate, by the unconquerable spirit of the brave.

"Great is the glory, for the strife is hard!"

C. D. H.
January 10, 1917.

# INTRODUCTION

## THE OLD REGIME IN EUROPE

ANYONE who seeks to understand the stirring period in which we are now living becomes quickly aware that he must first know the history of the French Revolution, a movement that inaugurated a new era, not only for France but for the world. The years from 1789 to 1815, the years of the Revolution and of Napoleon, effected one of the greatest and most difficult transitions of which history bears record, and to gain any proper sense of its significance one must have some glimpse of the background, some conception of what Europe was like in 1789. That background can only be sketched here in a few broad strokes, far from adequate to a satisfactory appreciation, but at least indicating the point of departure.

What was Europe in 1789? One thing, at least, it was not: it was not a unity. There were states of every size and shape and with every form of government. The States of the Church were theocratic; capricious and cruel despotism prevailed in Turkey; absolute monarchy in Russia, Austria, France, Prussia; constitutional monarchy in England; while there were various kinds of so-called republics — federal republics in Holland and Switzerland, a republic whose head was an elective king in Poland, aristocratic republics in Venice and Genoa and in the free cities of the Holy Roman Empire.

Of these states the one that was to be the most persistent enemy of France and of French ideas throughout the period we are about to describe was England, a commercial and colonial empire of the first importance. This empire, of long, slow growth, had passed through many highly significant experiences during the eighteenth century. Indeed, that century is one of the most momentous in English history, rendered forever memorable by three great series of events which in important respects transformed her national life and her international relations, giving them the character and tendency which have been theirs ever since. These three streams of tendency or lines of evolution out of which the modern power of Britain has emerged were: the acquisition of what are still the most valuable parts of her colonial empire, Canada and India; the establishment of the parliamentary system of government, that is, government of the nation by its representatives, not by its royal house, the undoubted supremacy of Parliament over the Crown; and the beginnings of what is called the Industrial Revolution, that is, of the modern factory system of production on a vast scale which during the course of the nineteenth century made England easily the chief industrial nation of the world.

The evolution of the parliamentary system of government had, of course, been long in progress but was immensely furthered by the advent in 1714 of a new royal dynasty, the House of Hanover, still at this hour the reigning family. The struggle between Crown and Parliament, which had been long proceeding and had become tense and violent in the seventeenth century in connection with the attempts of the Stuart kings to make the monarchy all-powerful and supreme, ended finally in the eighteenth century with the victory of Parliament, and the monarch ceased to be, what he remained in the rest of Europe, the dominant element in the state.

In 1701 Parliament, by mere legislative act, altered the line of succession by passing over the direct, legitimate claimant because he was a Catholic, and by calling to the throne George, Elector of Hanover, because he was a Protestant. Thus the older branch of the royal family was set aside and a younger or collateral branch was put in its place. This was a plain defiance of the ordinary rules of descent which generally underlie the monarchical system everywhere. It showed that the will of Parliament was superior to the monarchical principle, that, in a way, the monarchy was elective. Still other important consequences followed from this act.

George I, at the time of his accession to the English throne in 1714 fifty-four years of age, was a German. He continued to be a German prince, more concerned with his electorate of Hanover than with his new kingdom. He did not understand a word of English, and as his ministers were similarly ignorant of German, he was compelled to resort to a dubious Latin when he wished to communicate with them. He was king from 1714 to 1727, and was followed by his son, George II, who ruled from 1727 to 1760 and who, though he knew English, spoke it badly and was far more interested in his petty German principality than in imperial Britain.

The first two Georges, whose chief interest in England was the money they could get out of it, therefore allowed their ministers to carry on the government and they did not even attend the meetings of the ministers where questions of policy were decided. For forty-six years this royal abstention continued. The result was the establishment of a regime never seen before in any country. The royal power was no longer exercised by the king, but was exercised by his ministers, who, moreover, were members of Parliament. In other words, to use a phrase that has become famous, the king reigns but does not govern. Parliament really governs, through a committee of its members, the ministers.

The ministers must have the support of the majority party in Parliament, and during all this period they, as a matter of fact, relied upon the party of the Whigs. It had been the Whigs who had carried through the revolution of 1688 and who were committed to the principle of the limitation of the royal power in favor of the sovereignty of Parliament. As George I and George II owed their throne to this party, and as the adherents of the other great party, the Tories, were long supposed to be supporters of the discarded Stuarts, England entered upon a period of Whig rule, which steadily undermined the authority of the monarch. The Hanoverian kings owed their position as kings to the Whigs. They paid for their right to reign by the abandonment of the powers that had hitherto inhered in the monarch.

The change that had come over their position did not escape the attention of the monarchs concerned. George II, compelled to accept ministers he detested, considered himself "a prisoner upon the throne." "Your ministers, Sire," said one of them to him, "are but the instruments of your government." George smiled and replied, "In this country the ministers are king."

Besides the introduction of this unique form of government the other great achievement of the Whigs during this period was an extraordinary increase in the colonial possessions of England, the real launching of Britain upon her career as a world-power, as a great imperial state. This sudden, tremendous expansion was a result of the Seven Years' War, which raged from 1756 to 1763 in every part of the world, in Europe, in America, in Asia, and on the sea. Many nations were involved and the struggle was highly complicated, but two phases of it stand out particularly and in high relief, the struggle between England and France, and the struggle between Prussia on the one hand and Austria, France, and Russia on the other. The Seven Years' War remains a mighty landmark in the history of England and of Prussia, its two conspicuous beneficiaries.

England found in William Pitt, later Earl of Chatham, an incomparable leader, a great orator of a declamatory and theatrical type, an incorruptible statesman, a passionate patriot, a man instinct with energy, aglow with pride and confidence in the splendor of the destinies reserved for his country. Pitt infused his own energy, his irresistible driving power into every branch of the public service. Head of the ministry from 1757 to 1761, he aroused the national sentiment to such a pitch, he directed the national efforts with such contagious and imperious confidence, that he turned a war that had begun badly into the most glorious and successful that England had ever fought. On the sea, in India, and in America, victory after victory over the French rewarded the nation's extraordinary efforts. Pitt boasted that he alone could save the country. Save it he surely did. He was the greatest of war ministers, imparting his indomitable resolution to multitudes of others. No one, it was said, ever entered his office without coming out a braver man. His triumph was complete when Wolfe defeated Montcalm upon the Plains of Abraham.

By the Peace of Paris, which closed this epochal struggle, England acquired from France the vast stretches of Nova Scotia, Canada, and the region between the Alleghanies and the Mississippi River, and also acquired Florida from Spain. From France, too, she snatched at the same time supremacy in India. Thus England had become a veritable world-empire under the inspiring leadership of the "Great Commoner." Her horizons, her interests, had grown vastly more spacious by this rapid increase in military renown, in power, in territory. She had mounted to higher influence in the world, and that, too, at the expense of her old, historic enemy just across the Channel.

But all this prestige and greatness were imperiled and gravely compromised by the reign that had just begun. George III had, in 1760, come to the throne which he was not to leave until claimed by death sixty years later. "The name of George III," writes one English historian, "cannot be penned without a pang, can hardly be penned without a curse, such mischief was he fated to do the country." Unlike his two predecessors, he was not a German, but was a son of England, had grown up in England and had been educated there, and on his accession, at the age of twenty-two, had announced in his most famous utterance that he "gloried in the name of Briton." But wisdom is no birthright, and George III was not destined to show forth in his life the saving grace of that quality. With many personal virtues, he was one of the least wise of monarchs and one of the most obstinate.

His mother, a German princess, attached to all the despotic notions of her native land, had frequently said to him, "George, be a king." This maternal advice, that he should not follow the example of the first two Georges but should mix actively in public affairs, fell upon fruitful soil. George was resolved not only to reign but to govern in the good old monarchical way. This determination brought him into a sharp and momentous clash with the tendency and the desire of his age. The historical significance of George III lies in the fact that he was resolved to be the chief directing power in the state, that he challenged the system of government which gave that position to Parliament and its ministers, that he threw himself directly athwart the recent constitutional development, that he intended to break up the practices followed during the last two reigns and to rule personally as did the other sovereigns of the world. As the new system was insecurely established, his vigorous intervention brought on a crisis in which it nearly perished.

George III, bent upon being king in fact as well as in name, did not formally oppose the cabinet system of government, but sought to make the cabinet a. mere tool of his will, filling it with men who would take orders from him, and aiding them in controlling Parliament by the use of various forms of bribery and influence. It took several years to effect this real perversion of the cabinet system, but in the end the King absolutely controlled the ministry and the two chambers of Parliament. The Whigs, who since 1688 had dominated the monarch and had successfully asserted the predominance of Parliament, were gradually disrupted by the insidious royal policy, and were supplanted by the Tories, who were always favorable to a strong kingship and who now entered upon a period of supremacy which was to last until well into the nineteenth century.

After ten years of this mining and sapping the King's ideas triumphed in the creation of a ministry which was completely submissive to his will. This ministry, of which Lord North was the leading member, lasted twelve years, from 1770 to 1782. Lord North was minister after the King's own heart. He never pretended to be the head of the government, but accepted and executed the King's wishes with the ready obedience of a lackey. The royal autocracy was scarcely veiled by the mere continuance of the outer forms of a free government.

Having thus secured entire control of ministry and Parliament, George III proceeded to lead the British Empire straight toward destruction, to what Goldwin Smith has called "the most tragical disaster in English history." The King and his tools initiated a policy which led swiftly and inevitably to civil war. For the American Revolution was a civil war within the British Empire. The King had his supporters both in England and in America; he had opponents both in America and England. Party divisions were much the same in the mother country and in the colonies, Whigs versus Tories, the upholders of the principle of self-government against the upholders of the principle of the royal prerogative. In this appalling crisis not only was the independence of America involved, but parliamentary government has worked out in

England was also at stake. Had George III triumphed not only would colonial liberties have disappeared, but the right of Parliament to be predominant in the state at home would have vanished. The Whigs of England knew this well, and their leaders, Pitt, Fox, Burke, gloried in the victories of the rebellious colonists.

The struggle for the fundamental rights of free men, for that was what the American Revolution signified for both America and England, was long doubtful. France now took her revenge for the humiliations of the Seven Years' War by aiding the thirteen colonies, hoping thus to humble her arrogant neighbor, grown so great at her expense. It was the disasters of the American war that saved the parliamentary system of government for England by rendering the King unpopular, because disgracefully unsuccessful. In 1782 Lord North and all his colleagues resigned. This was the first time that an entire ministry had been overthrown.

George the Third's attempt to be master in the state had failed, and although the full consequences of his defeat did not appear for some time, nevertheless they were decisive for the future of England. The king might henceforth reign but he was not to govern. To get this cardinal principle of free government under monarchical forms established an empire was disrupted. From that disruption flowed two mighty consequences. The principles of republican government gained a field for development in the New World, and those of constitutional or limited monarchy a field in one of the famous countries of the Old. These two types of government have since exerted a powerful and an increasing influence upon other people's desirous of controlling their own destinies. Their importance as models worthy of imitation has not yet been exhausted.

But the disaster of the American war was so great that the immediate effect was a decided impairment of England's prestige. It is a curious fact that after that she was considered by most of the rulers of Europe a decaying nation. She had lost her most valuable colonies in America. The notion was prevalent that her successes in the Seven Years' War had not been due to her own ability but to the incapacity of Louis XV, whereas they had been due to both. The idea that it was possible to destroy England was current in France, the idea that her empire was really a phantom empire which would disappear at the first hostile touch, that India could be detached far more easily than the thirteen colonies had been. It was considered that as she had grown rich she had lost her virility and energy and was undermined by luxury and sloth. At the same time, although in flagrant contradiction to the sentiments just described, there was a vague yet genuine fear of her. Though she had received so many blows, yet she had herself in the past given so many to her rivals, and especially to France, that they did well to have a lurking suspicion after all as to her entire decadence. The rivalry, centuries old, of France and England was one of the chief elements of the general European situation. It had shown no signs of abating. The issues of the Revolution were to cause it to flame up portentously. It dominated the whole period down to Waterloo. In England the French Revolution was destined to find its most redoubtable and resolute enemy.

In Italy, on the other hand, it was to find, partly a receptive pupil, partly an easy prey. The most important thing about Italy was that it was unimportant. Indeed, there was no Italy, no united, single country, but only a collection of petty states, generally backward in their political and economic development. Once masters in their own house, the Italians had long ago fallen from their high estate and had for centuries been in more or less subjection to foreigners, to Spaniards, to Austrians, sometimes to the French. This had reacted unfavorably upon their characters, and had made them timid, time-serving, self-indulgent, pessimistic. They had no great attachment to their governments, save possibly in Piedmont and in the republics of Venice and Genoa, and there was no reason why they should have. Several of the governments were importations from abroad, or rather impositions, which had never struck root in the minds or interests of the peoples. The political atmosphere was one of indifference, weariness, disillusionment. However, toward the end of the eighteenth century there were signs of an awakening. The Italians could never long be unmindful of the glories of their past. They had their haunting traditions which would never allow them to forget or renounce their rights, however oppressed they might be. They were a people of imagination and of fire, though they long appeared to foreigners quite the reverse, as in fact the very stuff of which willing slaves are made, a view which was seriously erroneous. It cannot be said that there was in the eighteenth century any movement aiming at making Italy a nation, but there were poets and historians who flashed out, now and then, with some patriotic phrase or figure that revealed vividly a shining goal on the distant horizon toward which all Italians ought to press. "The day will come," said Alfieri, "when the Italians will be born again, audacious on the field of battle." Humanity was not meant to be shut in by such narrow horizons as those presented by these petty states, but was entitled to more spacious destinies. This longing for national unity was as yet the passion of only a few, of men of imagination who had a lively sense of Italy's great past and who also possessed an instinct for the future. A French writer expressed a mood quite general with cultivated people when she said: "The Italians are far more remarkable because of what they have been and because of what they might be than because of what they now are." Seeds of a new Italy were already germinating. They were not, however, to yield their fruit until well into the nineteenth century. Turning to the east of France we find Germany, the country that was to be the chief battlefield of Europe for many long years, and that was to undergo the most surprising transformations. Germany, like Italy, was a collection of small states, only these states were far more numerous than in the peninsula to the south. Germany had a form of unity, at least it pretended to have, in the so-called Holy Roman Empire. How many states were included in it, it is difficult to say; at least 360, if in the reckoning are included all the nobles who recognized no superior save the emperor, who held their power directly from him and were subject to no one else. There were more than fifty free or imperial cities, holding directly from the emperor and managing their own affairs; and numerous ecclesiastical states, all independent of each other. Then there were small states like Baden and Württemberg and Bavaria and many others. In all this empire there were only two states of any importance in the general affairs of Europe, Prussia and Austria.

This empire, with its high-sounding names, "Holy" and "Roman," was incredibly weak and inefficient. Its emperor, not hereditary but elective, was nothing but a pompous, solemn pretence. He had no real authority, could give no orders, could create no armies, could follow out no policies, good or bad, for the German princes had during the course of the centuries robbed him of all the usual and necessary attributes of power. He was little more than a gorgeous figure in a pageant. There were, in addition, an Imperial Diet or national assembly, and an imperial tribunal, but they were as palsied as was the emperor.

What was important in Germany was not the empire, which was powerless for defense, useless for any serious purpose, but the separate states that composed it, and indeed only a few of these had any significance. All these petty German princelings responded to two emotions. All were jealous of their independence and all were eager to annex each other's territory. They never thought of the interests of Germany, of the empire, of the Fatherland. What power they had they had largely secured by despoiling the empire. Patriotism was not one of their weaknesses. Each was looking out emphatically for himself. To make a strong, united nation out of such mutually repellent atoms would be nothing less than magical. The material was most unpromising. Nevertheless the feat has been accomplished, as we shall see, although, as in the case of Italy, not until well on into the nineteenth century.

The individual states were everything, the empire was nothing, and with it the French Revolutionists and Napoleon were destined to play great havoc. Two states, as has been said, counted particularly, Austria and Prussia, enemies generally, rivals always, allies sometimes. Austria was old and famous, Prussia really quite new but rapidly acquiring a formidable reputation. Then, as now, the former was ruled by the House of Hapsburg, the latter by the House of Hohenzollern. There was no Austrian nation, but there was the most extraordinary jumble of states and races and languages to be found in Europe, whose sole bond of union was loyalty to the reigning house. The Hapsburg dominions were widely, loosely scattered, though the main bulk of them was in the Danube valley. There was no common Austrian patriotism; there were Bohemians, Hungarians, Milanese, Netherlanders, Austrians proper, each with a certain sense of unity, a certain self-consciousness, but there was no single nation comprehending, fusing all these elements. Austria was not like France or England. Nevertheless there were twenty-four millions of people under the direction of one man, and therefore they were an important factor in the politics of Europe.

In the case of Prussia, however, we have a real though still rudimentary nation, hammered together by hard, repeated, well-directed blows delivered by a series of energetic, ambitious rulers. Prussia as a kingdom dated only from 1701, but the heart of this state was Brandenburg, and Brandenburg had begun a slow upward march as early as the fifteenth century, when the Hohenzollerns came from South Germany to take control of it. In the sixteenth century the possessions of this family were scattered from the region of the Rhine to the borders of Russia. How to make them into a single state, responsive to a single will, was the problem. In each section there were feudal estates, asserting their rights against their ruler. But the Hohenzollerns had a very clear notion of what they wanted. They wished and intended to increase their own power as rulers, to break down all opposition within, and without steadily to aggrandize their domains. In the realization of their program, to which they adhered tenaciously from generation to generation, they were successful. Prussia grew larger and larger, the government became more and more autocratic, and the emphasis in the state came to be more and more placed upon the army. Mirabeau was quite correct when he said that the great national industry of Prussia was war. Prussian rulers were hard-working, generally conceiving their mission soberly and seriously as one of service to the state, not at all as one inviting to personal self-indulgence. They were hard-headed and intelligent in developing the economic resources of a country originally little favored by nature. They were attentive to the opportunities afforded by German and European politics for the advancement of rulers who had the necessary intelligence and audacity. In the long reign of Frederick II, called the Great (1740-1786), and unquestionably far and away the ablest of all the rulers of the Hohenzollern dynasty, we see the brilliant and faithful expression of the most characteristic features, methods, and aspirations of this vigorous royal house.

The successive monarchs of Prussia justified the extraordinary emphasis they put upon military force by pointing to the fact that their country had no natural boundaries but was simply an undifferentiated part of the great sandy plain of North Germany, that no river or no mountain range gave protection, that the way of the invader was easy. This was quite true, but it was also equally true that Prussia's neighbors had no greater protection from her than she from them. As far as geography was concerned, invasion of Prussia was no easier than aggression from Prussia. At any rate every Prussian ruler felt himself first a general, head of an army which it was his pride to increase. Thus the Great Elector, who had ruled from 1640 to 1688, had inherited an army of less than 4,000 men, and had bequeathed one of 24,000 to his successor. The father of Frederick II had inherited one of 38,000 and had left one of 83,000. Thus Prussia with a population of two and a half millions had an army of 83,000, while Austria with a population of 24,000,000 had one of less than 100,000. With this force, highly drilled and amply provided with the sinews of war by the systematic and rigorous economies of his father, Frederick was destined to go far. He is one of the few men who have changed the face of Europe. By war, and the subsidiary arts that minister unto it, Frederick pushed his small state into the very forefront of European politics. Before his reign was half over he had made it one of the great powers, everywhere reckoned as such, although in population, area, and wealth, compared with the other great powers, it was small indeed.

As a youth all of Frederick's tastes had been for letters, for art, for music, for philosophy and the sciences, for conversation, for the delicacies and elegancies of culture. The French language and French literature were his passion and remained his chief source of enjoyment all through his life. He wrote French verses, he hated military exercises, he played the flute, he detested tobacco, heavy eating and drinking, and the hunt, which appeared to his father as the natural manly and royal pleasures. The thought that this youth, so indifferent or hostile to the stern, bleak, serious ideals of duty incumbent upon the royal house for the welfare of Prussia, so interested in the frivolities and fripperies of life, so carelessly self-indulgent, would one day be king and would probably wreck the state by his incompetence and his levity, so enraged the father, Frederick William I, a rough, boorish, tyrannical, hard-working, and intensely patriotic man, that he subjected the Crown Prince to a Draconian discipline which at times attained a pitch of barbarity, caning him in the presence of the army, boxing his ears before the common people, compelling him from a prison window to witness the execution of his most intimate friend, who had tried to help him escape from this odious tyranny by attempted flight from the country. In such a furnace was the young prince's mettle steeled, his heart hardened. Frederick came out of this ordeal self-contained, cynical, crafty, but sobered and submissive to the fierce paternal will. He did not, according to his father's expression, "kick or rear" again. For several years he buckled to the prosaic task of learning his future trade in the traditional Hohenzollern manner, discharging the duties of minor offices, familiarizing himself with the dry details of administration, and invested with larger responsibilities as his reformation seemed, in the eyes of his father, satisfactorily to progress.

When he came to the throne in 1740 at the age of twenty-eight he came equipped with a free and keen intellect, with a character of iron, and with an ambition that was soon to set the world in flame. He ruled for forty-six years and before half his reign was over it was evident that he had no peer in Europe. It was thought that he would adopt a manner of life quite different from his father's. Instead, however, there was the same austerity, the same simplicity, the same intense devotion to work, the same singleness of aim, that aim being the exaltation of Prussia. The machinery of government was not altered, but it was now driven at unprecedented speed by this vigorous, aggressive, supple personality. For Frederick possessed supreme ability and displayed it from the day of his accession to the day of his death. He was, as Lord Acton has said, "the most consummate practical genius that, in modern times, has inherited a throne."

His first important act revealed the character and the intentions of the ruler. For this man who as a youth had loathed the life of a soldier and had shirked its obligations as long as he could was now to prove himself one of the great military commanders of the world's history. He was the most successful of the robber barons in which the annals of Germany abounded, and he had the ethics of the class. He invaded Silesia, a large and rich province belonging to Austria and recognized as hers by a peculiarly solemn treaty signed by Prussia. But Frederick wanted it and considered the moment opportune as an inexperienced young woman, Maria Theresa, had just ascended the Austrian throne. "My soldiers were ready, my purse was full," said Frederick concerning this famous raid. Of all the inheritance of Maria Theresa "Silesia," said he, "was that part which was most useful to the House of Brandenburg." "Take what you can," he also remarked, "you are never wrong unless you are obliged to give back." In these utterances Frederick paints himself and his reign in imperishable colors. Success of the most palpable sort was his reward. Neither plighted faith, nor chivalry toward a woman, nor any sense of personal honor ever deterred him from any policy that might promise gain to Prussia. One would scarcely suspect from such hardy sentiments that Frederick had as a young man written a treatise against the statecraft of Machiavelli. That eminent Florentine would, it is safe to say, have been entirely content with the practical precepts according to which his titled critic fashioned his actual conduct. The true, authentic spirit of Machiavelli's political philosophy has never been expressed with greater brevity and precision than by Frederick. "If there is anything to be gained by being honest, honest we will be; and if it is necessary to deceive, let us be scoundrels."

If there is any defense for Frederick's conduct to be found in the fact that his principles or his lack of them were shared by most of his crowned contemporaries and by many other rulers before and since, he is entitled to that defense. He himself, however, was never much concerned about this aspect of the matter. It was, in his opinion, frankly negligible.

Frederick seized Silesia with ease in 1740, so unexpected was the attack. He thus added to Prussia a territory larger than Massachusetts, Connecticut, and Rhode Island combined, and a population of over a million and a quarter. But having seized it, he was forced to fight intermittently for twenty-three years before he could be sure of his ability to retain it. The first two Silesian wars (1740-1748) are best known in history as the wars of the Austrian Succession. The third was the Seven Years' War, a world conflict, as we have seen, involving most of the great states of Europe, but important to Frederick mainly because of its relation to his retention of Silesia.

It was the Seven Years' War (1756-1763) that made the name and fame of Frederick ring throughout the world. But that deadly struggle several times seemed about to engulf him and his country in utter ruin. Had England not been his ally, aiding with her subsidies and with her campaigns against France, in

Europe, Asia, America, and on the high seas, thus preventing that country from fully co-operating against Prussia, Frederick must have failed. The odds against him were stupendous. He, the ruler of a petty state with not more than 4,000,000 inhabitants, was confronted by a coalition of Austria, France, Russia, Sweden, and many little German states, with a total population perhaps twenty times as large as Prussia's. This coalition had already arranged for the division of his kingdom. He was to be left only Brandenburg, the primitive core of the state, the original territory given to the House of Hohenzollern in 1415 by the emperor.

Practically the entire continent was united against this little state which a short time before had hardly entered into the calculations of European politics. But Frederick was un-daunted. He overran Saxony, a neutral country, seized its treasury because he needed it, and, by a flagrant breach of international usage, forced its citizens to fight in his armies, which were thus considerably increased. When reproached for this unprecedented act he laconically replied that he rather prided himself on being original.

The war thus begun had its violent ups and downs. Attacked from the south by the Austrians, from the east by the Russians, and always outnumbered, Frederick, fighting a defensive war, owed his salvation to the rapidity of his manoeuvres, to the slowness of those of his enemies, to his generally superior tactics, and to the fact that there was an entire lack of co-ordination among his adversaries. He won the battle of Rossbach in 1757, his most brilliant victory, whose fame has not yet died away. With an army of only 20,000 he defeated a combined French and German army of 55,000 in an engagement that lasted only an hour and a half, took 16,000 prisoners, seventy-two cannon, and sustained a loss of less than a thousand men himself. Immense was the enthusiasm evoked by this Prussian triumph over what was reputed to be the finest army in Europe. It mattered little that the majority of the conquered army were Germans. The victory was popularly considered one of Germans over French, and such has remained its reputation ever since in the German national consciousness, thus greatly stirred and vivified.

Two years later Frederick suffered an almost equally disastrous defeat at the hands of the Austrians and Russians at Kunersdorf. "I have had two horses killed under me," he wrote the night after this battle, "and it is my misfortune that I still live myself. … Of an army of 48,000 men I have only 3,000 left. … I have no more resources and, not to lie about it, I think everything is lost."

Later, after another disaster, he wrote: "I should like to hang myself, but we must act the play to the end." In this temper he fought on, year after year, through elation, through depression, with defeat behind him and defeat staring him in the face, relieved by occasional successes, saved by the incompetence and folly of his enemies, then plunged in gloom again, but always fighting for time and for some lucky stroke of fortune, such as the death of a hostile sovereign with its attendant interruption or change of policy. The story is too crowded, too replete with incident, to be condensed here. Only the general impression of a prolonged, racking, desperate struggle can be indicated. Gritty, cool, alert, and agile, Frederick managed to hold on until his enemies were ready and willing to make peace.

He came out of this war with his territories intact but not increased. Silesia he retained, but Saxony he was forced to relinquish. He came out of it, also, prematurely old, hard, bitter, misanthropic, but he had made upon the world an indelible impression of his genius. His people had been decimated and appallingly impoverished; nevertheless he was the victor and great was his renown. Frederick had conquered Silesia in a month and had then spent many years fighting to retain it. All that he had won was fame, but that he enjoyed in full and overflowing measure.

Frederick lived twenty-three years longer, years of unremitting and very fruitful toil. In a hundred ways he sought to hasten the recuperation and the development of his sorely visited land, draining marshes, clearing forests, encouraging industries, opening schools, welcoming and favoring immigrants from other countries. Indeed, over 300,000 of these responded to the various inducements offered, and Frederick founded more than 800 villages. He reorganized the army, replenished the public treasury, remodeled the legal code. In religious affairs he was the most tolerant ruler in Europe, giving refuge to the Jesuits when they were driven out of Catholic countries France, Portugal, Spain and when their order was abolished by the Pope himself. "In Prussia," said he, "everyone has the right to win salvation in his own way."

In practice this was about the only indubitable right the individual possessed, for Frederick's government was unlimited, although frequently enlightened, despotism. His was an absolute monarchy, surrounded by a privileged nobility, resting upon an impotent mass of peasantry. His was a militarist state and only nobles could become general officers. Laborious, rising at three in summer, at four in the winter, and holding himself tightly to his mission as "first servant to the King of Prussia," Frederick knew more drudgery than pleasure. But he was a tyrant to his fingertips, and we do not find in the Prussia of his day any room made for that spirit of freedom which was destined in the immediate future to wrestle in Europe with this outworn system of autocracy.

In 1772 the conqueror of Silesia proceeded to gather new laurels of a similar kind. In conjunction with the monarchs of Russia and Austria he partially dismembered Poland, a crime of which the world has not yet heard the last. The task was easy of accomplishment, as Poland was defenseless. Frederick frankly admitted that the act was that of brigands, and his opinion has been ratified by the general agreement of posterity.

When Frederick died in 1786, at the age of seventy-four, he left his kingdom nearly doubled in size and with a population more than doubled. In all his actions he thought, not of Germany, but of Prussia, always Prussia. Germany was an abstraction that had no hold upon his practical mind. He considered the German language boorish, "a jargon, devoid of every grace," and he was sure that Germany had no literature worthy of the name. Nevertheless he was regarded throughout German lands, beyond Prussia, as a national hero, and he filled the national thought and imagination as no other German had done since Luther. His personality, his ideas, and his methods became an enduring and potent factor in the development of Germany.

But the trouble with despotism as a form of government is that a strong or enlightened despot may so easily be succeeded by a feeble or foolish one, as proved to be the case when Frederick died and was succeeded in 1786 by Frederick William II, under whom and under whose successor came evil days, contrasting most unpleasantly with the brilliant ones that had gone before.

Lying beyond Austria and Prussia, stretching away indefinitely into the east, was the other remaining great power in European politics, Russia.

Though the largest state on the continent, Russia did not enter upon the scene of European politics as a factor of importance until very late, indeed until the eighteenth century. During that century she took her place among the great European powers and her influence in the world has gone on increasing down to the present moment. Her previous history had been peculiar, differing in many and fundamental respects from that of her western neighbors. She had lived apart, unnoticed and unknown. She was connected with Europe by two ties, those of race and religion. The Russians were a Slavic people, related to the Poles, the Bohemians, the Serbs, and the other branches of that great family which spreads over eastern Europe. And as early as the tenth century they had been converted to Christianity, not to that form that prevailed in the West, but to the Orthodox Greek form, which had its seat in Constantinople. The missionaries who had brought religion and at the same time the beginnings of civilization had come from that city. After the conquest of Constantinople by the infidel Turks in 1453 the Russians considered themselves its legitimate heirs, the representatives of its ideas and traditions. Constantinople exercised over their imaginations a spell that has only increased with time.

But the great central fact of Russian history for hundreds of years was not her connection with Europe, which, after all, was slight, but her connection with Asia, which was close and profound in its effects. The Principality of Muscovy, as Russia was then called from its capital Moscow, was conquered by the Mongols, barbarians from Asia, in the thirteenth century, and for nearly three hundred years Russian princes paid tribute and made occasional visits of submission to the far-off Great Khan. Though constantly resenting this subjection, they did not escape its effects. They themselves became half-Asiatic. The men of Russia dressed in Oriental fashion, wearing the long robes with long sleeves, the turbans and slippers of the East. They wore their hair and beards long. The women were kept secluded and were heavily veiled when in public. A young girl saw her husband for the first time the day of her marriage. There was no such thing as society as we understand the term. The government was an Oriental tyranny, unrestrained, regardless of human life. In addressing the ruler a person must completely prostrate himself, his forehead touching the floor, a difficult as well as a degrading attitude for one human being to assume toward another.

In time the Russians threw off the Mongol domination, after terrible struggles, and themselves in turn conquered northern Asia, that is, Siberia. A new royal house came to the throne in 1613, the House of Romanoff, still the reigning family of Russia.

But the Russians continued to have only the feeblest connection with Europe, knowing little of its civilization, caring less, content to vegetate in indolence and obscurity. Out of this dull and laggard state they were destined to be roughly and emphatically roused by one of the most energetic rulers known to history, Peter the Great, whose reign of thirty-six years (1689-1725) marks a tremendous epoch, both by what it actually accomplished and by what it indicated ought to be the goal of national endeavor. As a boy Peter had been given no serious instruction, no training in self-control, but had been allowed to run wild, and had picked up all sorts of acquaintances and companions, many of them foreigners. It was the chance association with Europeans living in the foreign quarter of Moscow that proved the decisive fact of his life, shaping his entire career. From them he got a most irregular, haphazard, but original education, learning a little German, a little Dutch, some snatches of science, arithmetic, geometry. His chief boyish interest was in mechanics and its relation to the military art. With him, playing soldier was more serious than with most boys. He used to build wooden fortresses, surrounded with walls and moats and bastions. Some of his friends would defend the redoubt while he and the others attacked it. Sometimes lives were lost, always some were wounded. Such are the fortunes of war, though not usually of juvenile war. "The boy is amusing himself," was the comment of his sister, who was exercising the regency in his name. Passionately fond of military games, Peter was also absorbingly interested in boats and ships, and eagerly learned all he could of navigation, which was not much, for the arts of shipbuilding and navigation were in their very infancy in Russia.

Learning that his sister Sophia was planning to ignore his right to the throne and to become ruler herself, he dropped his sham rights and his sailing, swept his sister aside into a nunnery, and assumed control of the state. Convinced that Europe was in every way superior to Russia, that Russia had everything to gain and nothing to lose from a knowledge of the ways and institutions of the western countries, Peter's policy from the beginning to the end of his reign was to bring about the closest possible connection between his backward country and the progressive and brilliant civilization which had been built up in England, France, Holland, Italy, and Germany.

But even with the best intentions this was not an easy task. For Russia had no point of physical contact with the nations of western Europe. She could not freely communicate with them, for between her and them was a wall consisting of Sweden, Poland, and Turkey. Russia was nearly a land-locked country. Sweden controlled all that coast-line along the Baltic which is now Russian, Turkey controlled all the coast-line of the Black Sea. The only port Russia possessed was far to the north, at Archangel, and this was frozen during nine months of the year. To communicate freely and easily with the West, Russia must "open a window" somewhere, as Peter expressed it. Then the light could stream in. He must have an ice-free port in European waters. To secure this he fought repeated campaigns against Turkey and Sweden. With the latter power there was intermittent war for twenty years, very successful in the end, though only after distressing reverses. He conquered the Baltic Provinces from Sweden, Courland, Estonia, and Livonia, and thus secured a long coast-line. Russia might now have a navy and a merchant fleet and sea-borne commerce. "It is not land I want, but water," Peter had said. He now had enough, at least to begin with.

Meanwhile he had sent fifty young Russians of the best families to England, Holland, and Venice to learn the arts and sciences of the West, especially shipbuilding and fortifications. Later he had gone himself for the same purpose, to study on the spot the civilization whose superiority he recognized and intended to impose upon his own country, if that were possible. This was a famous voyage. Traveling under the strictest incognito, as "Peter Mikailovitch," he donned laborer's clothes and worked for months in the shipyards of Holland and England. He was interested in everything. He visited mills and factories of every kind, asking innumerable questions: "What is this for? How does that work?" He made a sheet of paper with his own hands. During his hours of recreation he visited museums, theaters, hospitals, galleries. He saw printing presses in operation, attended lectures on anatomy, studied surgery a little, and even acquired some proficiency in the humble and useful art of pulling teeth. He bought collections of laws, and models of all sorts of machines, and engaged many officers, mechanics, printers, architects, sailors, and workmen of every kind, to go to Russia to engage in the task of imparting instruction to a nation which, in Peter's opinion, needed it and should receive it, willy-nilly.

Peter was called home suddenly by the news of a revolt among the imperial troops devoted to the old regime and apprehensive of the coming innovations. They were punished with every refinement of savage cruelty, their regiments disbanded, and a veritable reign of terror preceded the introduction of the new system.

Then the Czar began with energy his transformation of Russia, as he described it. The process continued all through his reign. It was not an elaborate, systematic plan, deliberately worked out beforehand, but first this reform, then that, was adopted and enforced, and in the end the sum-total of all these measures of detail touched the national life at nearly every point. Some of them concerned manners and customs, others economic matters, others matters purely political. Peter at once fell upon the long beards and Oriental costumes, which, in his opinion, symbolized the conservatism of Old Russia, which he was resolved to shatter. Arming himself with a pair of shears, he himself clipped the liberal beards and mustaches of many of his nobles, and cut their long coats at the knee. They must set the style, and the style must be that of France and Germany. Having given this sensational exhibition of his imperial purpose, he then compromised somewhat, allowing men to wear their beards long, but only on condition of submitting to a graduated tax upon these ornaments. The approbation of the Emperor, the compulsion of fashion, combined with considerations of economy, rapidly wrought a surprising change in the appearance of the manhood of Russia. Barbers and tailors were stationed at the entrances of towns to facilitate the process by slashing the offending members until they conformed to European standards. Women were forbidden to wear the veil and were released from the captivity of the harem, or terem, as it was called in Russia. Peter had attended the "assemblies" of France and England and had seen men and women dancing and conversing together in public. He now ordered the husbands and fathers of Russia to bring their wives and daughters to all social entertainments. The adjustments were awkward at first, the women frequently standing or sitting stiffly apart at one end of the room, the men smoking and drinking by themselves at the other. But finally society as understood in Europe emerged from these temporary and amusing difficulties. Peter gave lessons in dancing to some of his nobles, having himself acquired that accomplishment while on his famous trip. They were expected, in turn, to pass the secret on to others.

The organs of government, national and local, were remodeled by the adoption of forms and methods known to Sweden, Germany, and other countries, and the state became more efficient and at the same time more powerful. The army was enlarged, equipped, and trained mainly in imitation of Germany. A navy was created and the importance of the sea to the general life of the nation gradually dawned upon the popular intelligence. The economic development of the country was begun, factories were established, mines were opened, and canals were cut. The church was brought into closer subjection to the state. Measures were taken against vagabondage and robbery, widely prevalent evils. Education of a practical sort was encouraged. The Julian calendar was introduced and is still in force, though the other nations of Europe have since adopted another and more accurate chronology. Peter even undertook to reform the language of Russia, striking out eight of the more cumbersome letters of the alphabet and simplifying the form of some of the others.

All these changes encountered resistance, resistance born of indolence, of natural conservatism, of religious scruples. Was it not impious for Holy Russia to abandon her native customs and to imitate the heretics of the West? But Peter went on smashing his way through as best he could, crushing opposition by fair means and by foul, for the quality of the means was a matter of indifference to him, if only they were successful. Here we have the spectacle of a man who, himself a semi-barbarian, was bent upon civilizing men more barbarous than he.

As the ancient capital, Moscow, was the stronghold of stiff conservatism, was wedded to the old ideas and customs, Peter resolved to build a new capital on the Baltic. There, on islands and marshes at the mouth of a river which frequently overflowed, he built at frightful cost in human life and suffering the city of St. Petersburg. Everything had to be created literally from the ground up. Forests of piles had to be driven into the slime to the solid earth beneath to furnish the secure foundations. Tens of thousands of soldiers and peasants were drafted for the work. At first they had no implements, but were forced to dig with sticks and carry the rubbish away in their coats. No adequate provisions were made for them; they slept unprotected in the open air, their food was insufficient and they died by thousands, only to be replaced by other thousands. All through the reign the desperate, rough process went on. The will of the autocrat, rich in expedients, triumphed over all obstacles. Every great landowner was required to build in the city a residence of a certain size and style. No ship might enter without bringing a certain quantity of stone for building purposes. St. Petersburg was cut by numerous canals, as were the cities of Holland. The Czar required the nobles to possess boats. Some of them, not proficient in the handling of these novel craft, were drowned. Toward the close of his reign Peter transferred the government to this city which stood on the banks of the Neva, a monument to his imagination, his energy, and his persistence, a city with no hampering traditions, with no past, but with only an untrammeled future, an appropriate expression of the spirit of the New Russia which Peter was laboring to create.

He was, indeed, a strange leader for a people which needed above all to shake itself free from what was raw and crude, he was himself so raw and crude. A man of violent passions, capable and guilty of orgies of dissipation, of acts of savage cruelty, hard and fiendish in his treatment even of those nearest to him, his sister, his wife, and his son, using willingly as instruments of progress the atrocious knout and wheel and stake, Peter was neither a model ruler, nor a model man. Yet, with all these traits of primal barbarism in his nature, he had many redeeming points. Good-humored, frank, and companionable under ordinary circumstances, he was entirely natural, as loyal in his friendships as he was bitter in his enmities. Masterful, titanic, there was in him a wild vitality, an immense energy, and he was great in the singleness of his aim. He did not succeed in transforming Russia; that could not be accomplished in one generation or in two. But he left an army of two hundred thousand men, he connected Russia with the sea by the coast-line of the Baltic, thus opening a contact with countries that were more advanced, intellectually and socially, and he raised a standard and started a tradition.

Then followed, upon his death, a series of mediocre rulers, under whom it seemed likely that the ground gained might be lost. But under Elizabeth (1741-1762) Russia played an important part in the Seven Years' War, thus showing her altered position in Europe, and with the advent of Catherine II (1762-1796) the process of Europeanizing Russia and of expanding her territories and magnifying her position in international politics was resumed with vigor and carried out with success.

Catherine was a German princess, the wife of the Czar Peter III, who, proving a worthless ruler, was deposed, after a reign of a few months, then done to death, probably with the connivance of his wife. Catherine became empress, and for thirty-four years ruled Russia with an iron hand. Fond of pleasure, fond of work, a woman of intellectual tastes, or at least pretensions, which she satisfied by intimate correspondence with Voltaire, Diderot, and other French philosophers of the day, being rewarded for her condescension and her favors by their enthusiastic praise of her as the "Semiramis of the North," Catherine passes as one of the enlightened despots of her century. Being of western birth, she naturally sympathized with the policy of introducing western civilization into Russia, and gave that policy her vigorous support.

But her chief significance in history is her foreign policy. Three countries, we have seen, stood between Russia and the countries of western Europe, Sweden, Poland, and Turkey. Peter had conquered the first and secured the water route by the Baltic. Catherine devoted her entire reign to conquering the other two.

The former she accomplished by infamous means and with rare completeness. By the end of her reign Poland had been utterly destroyed and Russia had pushed her boundaries far westward until they touched those of Prussia and Austria. Catherine was not able to dismember Turkey as Poland was dismembered, but she gained from her the Crimea and the northern shores of the Black Sea from the Caucasus to the Dniester. She had even dreamed of driving the Turk entirely from Europe and of extending her own influence down to the Mediterranean by the establishment of a Byzantine empire that should be dependent upon Russia. But any dream of getting to Constantinople was a dream indeed, as the troubled history of a subsequent century was to show. Henceforth, however, Europe could count on one thing with certainty, namely, that Russia would be a factor to be considered in any rearrangement of the map of the Balkan peninsula, in any determination of the Eastern question.

This rise of Russia, like the rise of Prussia, to a position of commanding importance, in European politics, was the work of the eighteenth century. Both were characteristic products of that age.

The more one examines in general the governments of Europe in the eighteenth century, and the policies which they followed or attempted to follow, the less is one impressed with either their wisdom or their morality. The control was everywhere in the hands of the few and was everywhere directed to the advantage of the few. The idea that it was the first duty of the state to assure, if possible, the welfare of the great majority of the people was not the idea recognized in actual practice. The first duty of the state was to increase its dominions by hook or crook, and to provide for the satisfaction of the rulers and the privileged classes. One could find in all Europe hardly a trace of what we call democracy. Europe was organized aristocratically, and for the benefit of aristocracies. This was true even in such a country as England, which had a parliament and established liberties; even in republics, like Venice or Genoa or the cantons of Switzerland.

The condition of the vast mass of the people in every country was the thing least considered. It was everywhere deplorable, though varying, more or less, in different countries. The masses, who were peasants, were weighed down and hemmed in by laws and institutions and customs that took no account of their well-being. In one way or another they were outrageously taxed, so that but a small fraction of what they earned went for their own support. Throughout most of Europe they did not possess what we regard as the mere beginnings of personal liberty, for, except in England and France, serfdom, with all its paralyzing restrictions, was in force. No one dreamed that the people were entitled to education so that they might be better equipped for life. The great substructure of European society was an unhappy, unfree, unprotected, undeveloped mass of human beings, to whom opportunity for growth and improvement was closed on every side.

If the governments of Europe did not seriously consider the interests of the most numerous and weakest class, on whose well-being depended absolutely the ultimate well-being of the nations, did they discharge their other obligations with any greater understanding or sense of justice? It cannot be said that they did. The distempers in every state were numerous and alarming. The writings of contemporaries abound in gloomy prophecies. There was a widespread feeling that revolutions, catastrophes, ruin were impending, that the body politic was nowhere in sound condition. Excessive expenditures for the maintenance of extravagant courts, for sumptuous buildings, for favorites of every stripe and feather, excessive expenditures for armies and for wars, which were frequent, resulted in increasing disorder in the finances of the various nations. States resorted more and more to loans, with the result that the income had to go for the payment of the interest. Deficits were chronic, and no country except England had a budget, or public and official statement of expenditures and receipts. Taxes were increasing and were detestably distributed. Everywhere in Europe the richer a man was the less he paid proportionately. As new taxes were imposed, exemptions, complete or partial, went with them, and the exemptions were for the nobility and, in part, for the middle classes, where such existed. Crushing therefore was the burden of the lower orders. It was truly a vicious circle.

These evils were so apparent that now and then they prompted the governing authorities to attempt reform. Several rulers in various countries made earnest efforts to improve conditions. These were the "benevolent despots" of the eighteenth century who tried reform from above before the French tried it from below. On the whole they had no great or permanent success, and the need of thoroughgoing changes remained to trouble the future.

Not only were the governments of Europe generally inefficient in all that concerned the full, symmetrical development of the economic, intellectual, and moral resources of the people, not only were they generally repressive and oppressive, allowing little scope to the principle of liberty, but they were, in their relations to each other, unprincipled, unscrupulous. The state was conceived as force, not at all as a moral being, subject to moral obligations and restraints. The glory of rulers consisted in extending the boundaries of their states, regardless of the rights of other peoples, regardless even of the rights of other rulers. The code that governed their relations with each other was primitive indeed. Any means were legitimate, success was the only standard of right or wrong. "He who gains nothing, loses," wrote Catherine of Russia, one of the "enlightened" despots. The dominant idea in all government circles was that the greatness of the state was in proportion to its territorial extent, not in proportion to the freedom, the prosperity, the education of its people. The prevalence of this idea brought it about that every nation sought to be ready to take advantage of any weakness or distress that might appear in the situation of its neighbors. Armies must be constantly at hand and diplomacy must be ready for any scurvy trick or infamous crime that might promise hope of gain. It followed that treaties were to be broken whenever there was any advantage in breaking them. "It is a mistake to break your word without reason," said Frederick II, "for thus you gain the reputation of being light and fickle." To keep faith with each other was no duty of rulers. There was consequently no certainty in international agreements.

This indifference to solemn promises was nothing new. The eighteenth century was full of flagrant violations of most explicit international agreements. There was no honor among nations. No state had any rights which any other state was bound to respect. These monarchs, "enlightened" and "benevolent" or not, as the case might be, all agreed that they ruled by divine right, by the will of God. Yet this decidedly imposing origin of their authority gave them no sense of security in their relations with each other, nor did it give to their reigns any exceptional purity or unworldly character. The maxims of statecraft which they followed were of the earth earthy. While bent upon increasing their own power they did not neglect the study of the art of undermining each other's power, however divinely buttressed in theory it might be. Monarchs were dethroned, states were extinguished, boundaries were changed and changed again, as the result of aggressive wars, during the eighteenth century. Moreover the wars of that time were famous for the exactions of the victors and for the scandalous fortunes made by some of the commanders. It was not the French Revolutionists nor was it Napoleon who introduced these customs into Europe. They could not, had they tried, have lowered the tone of war or statecraft in Europe. At the worst they might only imitate their predecessors.

The Old Regime in Europe was to be brought tumbling down in unutterable confusion as a result of the storm which was brewing in France and which we are now to study. But that regime had been undermined, the props that supported it had been destroyed, by its own official beneficiaries and defenders. The Old Regime was disloyal to the very principles on which it rested, respect for the established order, for what was old and traditional, for what had come down from the past, regard for legality, for engagements, loyalty to those in authority. How little regard the monarchs of Europe themselves had for principles which they were accustomed to pronounce sacred, for principles in which alone lay their own safety, was shown by the part they played in the great events of the eighteenth century already alluded to, the war of the Austrian Succession, and the Partition of Poland. By the first the ruler of Austria, Maria Theresa, was robbed of the large and valuable province of Silesia by Prussia, aided by France, both of which states had recently signed a peculiarly solemn treaty called the Pragmatic Sanction, by which her rights had been explicitly and emphatically recognized. Frederick II, however, wanted the province, took it, and kept it. This case shows how lightly monarchs regarded legal obligations, when they conflicted with their ambitions.

The other case, the Partition of Poland, was the most iniquitous act of the century. Poland was in geographical extent the largest state in Europe, next to Russia. Its history ran far back. But its government was utterly weak. Therefore in 1772 Prussia, Austria, and Russia attacked it for no cause save their own cupidity, and tore great fragments away, annexing them to their own territories. Twenty years later they completed the process in two additional partitions, in 1793 and 1795, thus entirely annihilating an ancient state. This shows how much regard the monarchs of Europe had for established institutions, for established authorities.

Two things only counted in Old Europe — force and will, the will of the sovereign. But force and will may be used quite as easily for revolution, for the overthrow of what is old and sacred, as for its preservation. There need be no surprise at anything that we may find Napoleon doing. He had a sufficient pattern and exemplar in Frederick the Great and in Catherine of Russia, only recently deceased when his meteoric career began.

The eighteenth century attained its legitimate climax in its closing decade, a very memorable period in the history of the world. The Old Regime in Europe was rudely shattered by the overthrow of the Old Regime in France, which country, by its astonishing actions, was to dominate the next quarter of a century.

# CHAPTER I

## THE OLD REGIME IN FRANCE

THE French Revolution brought with it a new conception of the state, new principles of politics and of society, a new outlook upon life, a new faith which seized the imagination of multitudes, inspiring them with intense enthusiasm, arousing boundless hopes, and precipitating a long and passionate struggle with all those who feared or hated innovation, who were satisfied with things as they were, who found their own conditions of life comfortable and did not wish to be disturbed. Soon France and Europe were divided into two camps, the reformers and the conservatives, those believing in radical changes along many lines and those who believed in preserving what was old and tried, either because they profited by it or because they felt that men were happier and more prosperous in living under conditions and with institutions to which they were accustomed than under those that might be ideally more perfect but would at any rate be strange and novel and uncertain.

In order to understand the French Revolution it is necessary to examine the conditions and institutions of France out of which it grew; in other words, the Old Regime. Only thus can we get our sense of perspective, our standard of values and of criticism. The Revolution accomplished a sweeping transformation in the life of France. Putting it in a single phrase it accomplished the transition from the feudal system of the preceding centuries to the democratic system of the modern world. The entire structure of the French state and of French society was remodeled and planted on new and far-reaching principles.

The essence of the feudal system was class divisions and acknowledged privileges for all classes above the lowest. The essence of the new system is the removal of class distinctions, the abolition of privileges, the introduction of the principle of the equality of men, wherever possible.

What strikes one most in contemplating the Old Regime is the prevalence and the oppressiveness of the privileges that various classes enjoyed. Society was simply honeycombed with them. They affected life constantly and at every point. It is not an easy society to describe in a few words, for the variations were almost endless. But, broadly speaking, and leaving details aside, French society was graded from top to bottom, and each grade differed, in legal rights, in opportunities for enjoyment and development, in power.

The system culminated in the monarch, the lofty and glittering head of the state, the embodiment of the might and the majesty of the nation. The king claimed to rule by the will of God, that is, by divine right, not at all by the consent of the people. He was responsible to no one but God. Consequently in the actual conduct of his office he was subject to no control. He was an absolute monarch. He could do as he chose. It was for the nation to obey. The will of the king and that alone was, in theory, the only thing that counted. It determined what the law should be that should govern twenty-five million Frenchmen in their daily lives. "This thing is legal because I wish it," said Louis XVI, thus stating in a single phrase the nature of the monarchy, the theory, and the practice also, if the monarch happened to be a strong man. The king made the laws, he levied the taxes, he spent them as he saw fit, he declared wars, made peace, contracted alliances according to his own inclination. There was in theory no restriction upon his power, and all his subjects lay in the hollow of his hand. He could seize their property; he could imprison them by a mere order, a lettre de cachet, without trial, and for such a period as he desired; he could control, if not their thoughts, at least the expression of them, for his censorship of the press, whether employed in the publication of books or newspapers, could muzzle them absolutely.

So commanding a figure required a broad and ample stage for the part he was to play, a rich and spacious background. Never was a being more sumptuously housed. While Paris was the capital of France, the king resided twelve miles away amid the splendors of Versailles. There he lived and moved and had his being in a palace that was the envy of every other king in Christendom, a monumental pile, with its hundreds of rooms, its chapel, theater, dining halls, salons, and endless suites of apartments for its distinguished occupants, the royal family, its hundreds of servants and its guests. This mammoth residence had been built a century before at an expense of about a hundred million dollars in terms of our money today, an imposing setting for a most brilliant and numerous court, lending itself, with its miles of corridors, of walks through endless formal gardens studded with statues, fountains, and artificial lakes, to all the pomp and pageantry of power. For the court which so dazzled Europe was composed of 18,000 people, perhaps 16,000 of whom were attached to the personal service of the king and his family, 2,000 being courtiers, the favored guests of the house, nobles who were engaged in a perpetual round of pleasures and who were also busily feathering their own nests by soliciting, of course in polished and subtle ways, the favors that streamed from a lavish throne. Luxury was everywhere the prevailing note. Well may the occupants of the palace have considered themselves, in spirit and in truth, the darlings of the gods, for earth had not anything to show more costly. The king, the queen, the royal children, the king's brothers and sisters and aunts all had their separate establishments under the spacious roof. The queen alone had 500 servants. The royal stables contained nearly 1,900 horses and more than 200 carriages, and the annual cost of this service alone was the equivalent of $4,000,000. The king's own table cost more than a million and a half. As gaiety was unconfined, so necessarily was the expenditure that kept it going, for everyone in this household secured what, in the parlance of our vulgar democracy, is called a handsome "rake-off." Thus ladies-in-waiting secured about $30,000 each by the privilege they enjoyed of selling the candles that had once been lighted but not used up. Queen Marie Antoinette had four pairs of shoes a week, which constituted a profitable business for somebody. In 1789 the total cost of all this riot of extravagance amounted to not far from $20,000,000. No wonder that men spoke of the court as the veritable nation's grave.

Not only were the King's household expenses pitched to this exalted scale, but, in addition, he gave money or appointments or pensions freely, as to the manner born, to those who gained his approbation and his favor. It has been estimated that in the fifteen years between 1774, when Louis XVI came to the throne, and 1789, when the whirlwind began, the King thus presented to favorites the equivalent of more than a hundred million dollars of our money. For those who basked in such sunshine it was unquestionably a golden age.

Such was the dazzling apex of a state edifice that was rickety in the extreme. For the government of France was ill-constructed and the times were decidedly out of joint. That government was not a miracle of design, but of the lack of it. Complicated, ill-adjusted, the various branches dimly defined or overlapping, it was thoroughly unscientific and inefficient. The king was assisted by five councils which framed the laws, issued the orders, conducted the business of the state, domestic and foreign, at the capital. Then for purposes of local government France was split up into divisions, but, unfortunately, not into a single, simple set. There were forty "governments," so called, thirty-two of which corresponded closely to the old provinces of France, the outcome of her feudal history. But those forty "governments" belied their name. They did little governing, but they furnished many lucrative offices for the higher nobility who were appointed "governors" and who resided generally in Versailles, contributing their part to the magnificent ceremonial of that showy parade ground.

The real, prosaic work was done in the thirty-six "generalities," as another set of divisions was called. Over each of these was an intendant who was generally of the middle or bourgeois class, accustomed to work. These intendants were appointed by the king to carry on the royal government, each in his own district. They generally did not originate much, but they carried out the orders that came from the capital and made their reports to it. Their power was practically unrestricted. Upon them depended in large measure the happiness or the misery of the provinces. Judging from the fact that most of them were very unpopular, it must be admitted that this, the real working part of the national government, did not contribute to the welfare of the people. The intendants were rather the docile tools of the misgovernment which issued from the five councils which were the five fingers of the king. As the head is, so are the members, and the officials under the intendants for the smaller local areas enjoyed the disesteem evoked by the oppressive or unjust policies of their superiors.

Speaking broadly, local self-government did not exist in France, but the local, like the national, government was directed and determined in Versailles. Were a bridge to be repaired over some little stream hundreds of miles from Paris, were a new roof required for a village church, the matter was regulated from Paris, after exasperating delay. It was the reign of the red tape in every sense of the word. The people stood like dumb, driven cattle before this monstrous system. The only danger lay in the chance that they might not always remain dumb. Here obviously was no school for popular political education a fact which explains many of the mistakes and failures of the people when, in the Revolution, they themselves undertook to rule, the monarchy having failed egregiously to discharge its functions either efficiently or beneficently.

Let no one suppose that because France was a highly centralized monarchy, culminating in the person of the king, that therefore the French government was a real unity. Nothing could be further from the truth. To study in detail the various aspects of the royal government, its divisions and subdivisions, its standards, its agents, its methods of procedure, is to enter a lane where the mind quickly becomes hopelessly bewildered, so great was the diversity in the machinery employed, so varied were the terms in use. Uniformity was nowhere to be seen. There was unity in the person of the king, necessarily, and there only. Everywhere else disunity, diversity, variety, without rhyme or reason. It would take a volume or many volumes to make this clear — even then the reader would be driven to despair in attempting to form a true mental picture of the situation. The institutions of France were a hodgepodge — chaos erected into a system, with no loss of the chaotic, and with no system. Nowadays the same laws, the same taxes, the same weights and measures prevail throughout the length and breadth of the land. But in 1789 no such simplicity or equality prevailed. Weights and measures had different names and different values as one moved from province to province, sometimes as one moved from village to village. In some provinces taxes were, not determined, but at least distributed, by certain people of the province. In other cases this distribution was effected directly by the agents of the king, that is, by the central government. In some parts of France the civil laws, that is, the laws that regulated the relations of individuals with each other, not with the state, were of Roman origin or character. There the written law prevailed. In other sections, however, mainly in the north, one changed laws, Voltaire said, as one changed post-horses. In such sections the laws were not written but were customary, that is, feudal in origin and in spirit. There were indeed 285 different codes of customary laws in force, that is 285 different ways of regulating legally the personal relations of men with men, within the confines of France.

Again the same diversity in another sphere. Thirteen of the provinces of central France enjoyed free trade, that is, merchandise could move freely from one end of that area to the other without restriction. But the other nineteen provinces were separated from each other, just as nations are, by tariff boundaries, and when goods passed from one such province to another, they passed through custom-houses and duties were paid on them, as on goods that come from Europe to the United States.

All these diversities in laws, all these tariff boundaries, are easily explained. They were historical survivals, troublesome and irritating reminders of the Middle Ages. As the kings of France had during the ages annexed this province and then that, they had, more or less, allowed the local customs and institutions to remain undisturbed. Hence this amazing patch-work which baffles description.

One consequence of all this was the persistence in France of that feeling which in American history is known as the states-rights feeling. While all admitted that they were Frenchmen, provincial feeling was strong and frequently assertive. Men thought of themselves as Bretons, as Normans, were attached to the things that differentiated them, were inflexible or stubborn opponents of all attempts at amalgamation. Before France could be considered strongly united, fusion on a grand scale had to be accomplished. This was to be one of the memorable and durable achievements of the Revolution.

The financial condition of this extravagant and inefficient state was deplorable and dangerous. Almost half of the national income was devoted to the payment of interest on the national debt. Expenditures were always larger than receipts, with the result that there was an annual deficit which had to be met by contracting a new loan, thus enlarging the debt and the interest charges. It appeared to be the principle of state finance that expenditures should not be determined by income but income should be determined by expenditure. The debt therefore constantly increased, and to meet the chronic deficit the government had recourse to well-known methods which only aggravated the evil — the sale of offices, new loans. During twelve years of the reign of Louis XVI, from 1776 to 1788, the debt increased nearly $600,000,000. People became unwilling to loan to the state, and it was practically impossible to increase the taxes. The national finances were in a highly critical condition. Bankruptcy impended, and bankruptcy can only be avoided in two ways, either by increasing receipts or by reducing expenditures, or both. Attempts were made in the one direction and in the other, but were ineffectual.

The receipts, of course, came from the taxes, and the taxes were already very burdensome, at least for those who paid them. They were of two kinds, the direct and the indirect. The direct taxes were those on real estate, on personal property, and on income. From some of these the nobles and the clergy were entirely exempt, and they therefore fell all the more heavily upon the class that remained, the third estate. From others the nobles, though not legally exempted, were in practice largely freed, because the authorities did not assess noble property nearly as high as they did the property of commoners. Tax-assessors stood in awe of the great. Thus the royal princes, who were subject to the income tax and who ought to have paid nearly two and a half million francs, as a matter of fact paid less than two hundred thousand. Again, a marquis who ought to have paid a property tax of 2,500 francs paid 400 and a bourgeois in the same province who ought to have paid 70 in reality paid 760. Such crass favoritism, which always worked in favor of the nobles, never in favor of members of the third estate, naturally served only deeply to embitter the latter class. Those who were the wealthiest and therefore the best able to support the state were the very ones who paid the least, thus conforming to the principle that to those that have shall be given and from those that have not shall be taken away even that which they have. It has been estimated that the state took from the middle classes, and from the workingmen and peasants, half their annual earnings in the form of these direct taxes.

There was another branch of the system of taxation which was oppressive and offensive for other reasons. There were certain indirect taxes which were collected, not by state officials but by private individuals or companies, the farmers of taxes, as they were called, who paid a lump sum to the state and then themselves collected the taxes, seeking of course to extract as much as possible from the people. Not only has this system of tax-collecting always proved most hateful, both in ancient and modern times, as the tax-farmers have always, in order to make as much as possible, applied the screws with pitiless severity, thus generating a maximum of odium and hatred; but in this particular case several of the indirect taxes would have been unjust and oppressive, even if collected with leniency, a thing never heard of. There was, for instance, the salt tax, or gabelle, which came home, in stark odiousness, to everyone. The trade in salt was not open to anyone who might wish to engage in it, but was a monopoly of a company that bought the privilege from the state, and that company was most astoundingly favored by the law. For every person above seven years of age was required to buy at least seven pounds of salt annually whether he wished it or not. Even the utterly poor, who had not money enough to buy bread, were severely punished if they refused or neglected to buy the stated amount of salt. Moreover the tax-collectors had the right to search all houses from top to bottom to see that there was no evasion. Illicit trade in this necessary commodity was incessantly tracked down and severely punished. On the very eve of the Revolution it was officially estimated that 20,000 persons were annually imprisoned and over 500 annually condemned to death, or to service in the galleys, which was hardly preferable, for engaging in the illegal trade in salt.

Moreover by an extra refinement in the art of oppression the seven pounds that all must buy could be used only for cooking or on the table. If one desired to salt down fish or meats for preservation, one must not use this particular salt for that purpose, but must buy an additional amount.

There was another equally intolerable tax, the excise on wine. The making of wine was a great national industry which had existed for centuries, but if ever there was a system calculated to depress it, it was the one in vogue in France. Wine was taxed all along the line from the producer to the consumer. Taxed at the moment of manufacture, taxed at the moment of sale by the producer, it was also taxed repeatedly in transportation, — thirty-five or forty times, for instance, between the south of France and Paris, so that the combined taxes amounted in the end to nearly as much as the cost of the original production. A trade exposed to such constant and heavy impositions could not greatly flourish.

Again the taxes both on salt and on wine were not uniform, but varied from region to region, so that the sense of unjust treatment was kept alive every day in the ordinary course of business, and so that smuggling was in many cases extremely profitable. This in turn led to savage punishments, which only augmented the universal discontent and entered like iron into the souls of men. In the system of taxation, as in the political structure, we find everywhere inequality of treatment, privileges, arbitrary and tyrannical regulations, coupled with uncertainty from year to year, for the regulations were not infrequently changed. No wonder that men, even nobles, criticised this fiscal system as shockingly unjust and scandalously oppressive.

The social organization of France, also, was far from satisfactory. On even the most cursory view many notorious abuses, many intolerable grievances, many irritating or harmful maladjustments stood forth, condemned by reason or the interest of large sections of the population. Forms outworn, and institutions from which the life had departed, but whence issued a benumbing influence, hampered development in many directions. French society was frankly based upon the principle of inequality. There were three classes or orders, the clergy, the nobility, and the third estate. Not only were the two former classes privileged, that is, placed upon a better footing than the last, but it is curious to observe how the pervasive principle of unequal rights broke up even the formal unity of each of these classes. There was inequality of classes and there was also inequality between sections of the same class. The two privileged orders were favored in many ways, such as complete or partial exemption from taxes, or the right themselves to tax — the clergy through its right to tithes, the nobility through its right to exact feudal dues. Even some of the members of the third estate enjoyed privileges denied the rest. There were classes within classes. Of the 25,000,000 of Frenchmen the clergy numbered about 130,000, the nobility 140,000, while possibly about as many bourgeois as these two combined enjoyed privileges that separated them from the mass of their class. Thus the privileged as a whole numbered less than 600,000, while the unprivileged numbered well over 24,000,000. One man in forty therefore belonged to the favored minority whose lot was differentiated from that of their fellowmen by artificial advantages and distinctions.

The clergy of the Roman Catholic Church formed the first order in the state. It was rich and powerful. It owned probably a fifth of the land of France. This land yielded a large revenue, and, in addition, the clergy exacted tithes on all the agricultural products of the realm. This was in reality a form of national taxation, with this difference from the other forms, that the proceeds went, not to the nation, but to the church. The church had still another source of income, the dues which it exacted as feudal landlord from those to whom it stood in that relation. The total income of this corporation was approximately $100,000,000 of our money. Out of this it was the duty of the church to maintain religious edifices and services, to support many hospitals and schools, to relieve personal distress by charity, for there was no such thing in France as organized poor relief by the state or municipality. Thus the church was a state within the state, performing several functions which in most modern societies are performed by the secular authority. This rich corporation was relieved from taxation. Although from time to time it paid certain lump sums to the national treasury, these were far smaller than they would have been had the church been taxed on its property and on its income in the same proportion as were the commoners.

An income so large, had it been wisely and justly expended, might have aroused no criticism, for many of the services performed by this organization were essential to the well-being of France. But here as elsewhere in the institutions of the country we find gross favoritism and wanton extravagance, which shocked the moral sense of the nation and aroused its indignation, because they belied so completely pretensions to a peculiar sanctity on which the church based its claims to its privileged position. For the organization did not treat its own staff with any sense of fair play. Much the larger part of the income went to the higher clergy, that is, to the 134 bishops and archbishops, and to a small number of abbots, canons, and other dignitaries — in all probably not more than 5,000 or 6,000 ecclesiastics. These highly lucrative positions were monopolized by the younger sons of the nobility, who were eager to accept the salaries but not disposed to perform the duties. Many of them resided at court and lived the gay and worldly life, with scarcely anything, save some slight peculiarity of dress, to indicate their ecclesiastical character. The morals of many were scandalous and their intellectual ability was frequently mediocre. They did not consider themselves men set apart for a high and noble calling, they did not take their duties seriously — of course there were honorable exceptions, yet they were exceptions — but their aims were distinctly finite and they conducted themselves as typical men of the world, attentive to the problem of self-advancement, devoted to all the pleasures, dissipations, and intrigues of Versailles. Some held several offices at once, discharging the obligations of none, and enjoying princely revenues. The Archbishop of Strassburg had an income of $300,000 a year and held high court in a splendid palace, entertaining 200 guests at a time. Even the saucepans of his kitchens were of silver. A hundred and eighty horses were in his stables, awaiting the pleasure of the guests.

A few of the bishops received small incomes, but the average among them was over $50,000 a year. They were in the main absentees, residing, not in their dioceses, but in Versailles, where further plums were to be picked up by the lucky, and where at any rate life was gay. Some of the bishoprics had even become the hereditary possessions of certain families, passing from uncle to nephew, as in the secular sphere many offices passed from father to son.

On the other hand, the lower clergy, the thousands of parish priests, who did the real work of spiritual consolation and instruction, who labored faithfully in the vineyard, were wretchedly requited. They were sons of the third estate, while their proud and prosperous superiors were sons of the nobility, and they were treated as plebeians. With wretched incomes of a few hundred francs, they had difficulty in keeping body and soul together. No wonder they were discontented and indignant, exclaiming that their lot "made the very stones and beams of their miserable dwellings cry aloud." No wonder they were bitter against their superiors, who neglected and exploited them with equal indifference. The privileged order of the clergy is thus seen to be divided into two classes, widely dissimilar in position, in origin, and in outlook upon life. The parish priests came from the people, experienced the hardships and sufferings of the people, saw the injustice of the existing system, and sympathized with plans for its reform. The clergy was divided into two classes. The triumph of the popular cause in the Revolution was powerfully aided by the lower clergy, who threw in their lot with the third estate at critical moments and against their clerical superiors, who rallied to the support of the absolute monarchy which had been so indulgent and so lavish to them. A house divided against itself, however, cannot permanently stand.

Somewhat similar was the situation of the second order, the nobility. As in the case of the clergy, there was here also great variety of condition among the members of this order, although all were privileged. There were several subdivisions, clearly enough marked. There were two main classes, the nobility of the sword and the nobility of the robe, that is, the old military nobility of feudal origin and the new judicial nobility, which secured its rank from the judicial offices its members held. The nobility of the sword consisted of the nobles of the court and of the nobles of the provinces. The former were few in number, perhaps a thousand, but they shone with peculiar brilliancy, for they were the ones who lived in Versailles, danced attendance upon the king, vied with each other in an eager competition for appointments in the army and navy and diplomatic service, for pensions and largesses from the royal bounty. These they needed, as they lived in a luxurious splendor that taxed their incomes and overtaxed them. Residing at court, they allowed their estates to be administered by bailiffs or stewards, who exacted all that they could get from the peasantry who cultivated them. Everybody was jealous of the nobles of this class, for they were the favored few, who practically monopolized all the pleasant places in the sun.

The contrast was striking between them and the hundred thousand provincial nobles who for various reasons did not live at court, were not known to the king, received no favors, and who yet were conscious that in purity of blood, in honorableness of descent and tradition, they were the equals or superiors of those who crowded about the monarch's person. Many of them had small incomes, some pitifully small. They could cut no figure in the world of society, they had few chances to increase their prosperity, which, in fact, tended steadily to decrease. Their sons were trained for the army, the only noble profession, but could never hope to rise very high because all the major appointments went to the assiduous suitors of the clique at court. They resided among the peasants and in some cases were hardly distinguishable from them, except that they insisted upon maintaining the tradition of their class, their badge of superiority, a life of leisure. To work was to lose caste. This obliged many of them to insist rigorously upon the payment of the various feudal dues owed them by the peasantry, some of which were burdensome, most of which were irritating. In some parts of France, however, as in the Vendee and in Brittany, they were sympathetic and helpful in their relations with the peasants and were in turn treated with respect by them.

The nobility as a whole enjoyed one privilege that was a serious and unnecessary injury to the peasants, making harder the conditions of their lives, always hard enough, namely the exclusive right of hunting, considered the chief noble sport. This meant in actual practice that the peasants might not disturb the game, although the game was destroying their crops. This was an unmitigated abuse, universally execrated by them.

The odium that came to be attached in men's minds to the nobility was chiefly felt only for the selfish and greedy minority. The provincial nobility, like the lower clergy, were themselves discontented with the existing order, for abundant reasons. They might not wish a sweeping transformation of society, but they were disposed to favor political reforms that would at least give all within the order an approximately equal chance. They were devoted to the king, but they experienced in their own persons the evils of an arbitrary and capricious government which was highly partial in its favors.

There was yet another section of the nobility whose status and whose outlook were different still. Many offices in France could be bought. They and their perquisites became the property of those who purchased them and could transmit them to their children, and one of the perquisites that such offices carried was a patent of nobility. This was the created nobility, the nobility of the robe, so called because its most conspicuous members were the judges, or members of the higher tribunals or parliaments. These judges appeared, in one aspect, as liberals, in that as lawyers they opposed certain unpopular innovations attempted by the king. But in reality as soon as their own privileges were threatened they became the stiffest of defenders of many of the most odious abuses of the Old Regime. In the opening days of the Revolution the Third Estate found no more bitter opponents than these ennobled judges.

Such were the two privileged orders. The rest of the population, comprising the vast majority of the people, was called the third estate. Differing from the others in that it was unprivileged, it resembled them in that it illustrated the principle of inequality, as did they. There were the widest extremes in social and economic conditions. Everyone who was not a noble nor a clergyman was a member of the third estate, the richest banker, the most illustrious man of letters, the poorest peasant, the beggar in the streets. Not at all homogeneous, the three chief divisions of this immense mass were the bourgeoisie, the artisans, and the peasants.

The bourgeoisie, or upper middle class, comprised all those who were not manual laborers. Thus lawyers, physicians, teachers, literary men were bourgeois: also merchants, bankers, manufacturers. Despite great national reverses, the bourgeoisie had grown richer during the past century as commerce had greatly increased. This economic growth had benefited the bourgeoisie almost exclusively, and many large fortunes had been built up and the general level of material welfare had been distinctly raised. These were the practical business men who loaned money to the state and who were frequently appointed to offices where business ability was required. Intelligent, energetic, educated, and well-to-do, this class resented most keenly the existing system. For they were made to feel in numerous galling ways their social inferiority, and, conscious that they were quite as well educated, quite as well-mannered as the nobles, they returned the disdain of the latter with envy and hatred. Having loaned immense sums to the state, they were increasingly apprehensive, as they saw it verging rapidly toward bankruptcy, because their interests were greatly imperiled. They therefore favored a political reorganization which should enable them to participate in the government, to control its expenditures, to assure its solvency, that thus they might be certain of their interest and principal, that thus abuses which impeded or injured business might be redressed, and that the precariousness of their position might be remedied.

They wished also a social revolution. Well educated, saturated with the literature of the period, which they read with avidity, their minds fermented with the ideas of Voltaire, Rousseau, Montesquieu, and the economists. Personally, man for man, they were as cultivated as the nobles. They wished social equality, they wished the laws to recognize what they felt the facts proved, that the bourgeois was the equal of the noble. They chafed under pretensions which they felt unjustified by any real superiority. Their mood was brilliantly expressed by a pamphlet written by one of their members, the Abbe Sieyes, which circulated enormously on the eve of the Revolution. "What is the Third Estate?" asked Sieyes. "Everything. What has it been in politics until now? Nothing. What does it desire? To become something."

Belonging to this estate but beneath the bourgeoisie were the artisans — perhaps two million and a half, living in the towns and cities. They were a comparatively small class because the industrial life of France was not yet highly developed. They were generally organized in guilds which had their rules and privileges that gave rise to bickerings galore and that were generally condemned as preventing the free and full expansion of industry and as artificially restricting the right to work.

The other large division of the third estate was the peasantry. This was by far the largest section. Indeed it was the nation. France was an agricultural country, more than nine-tenths of the population were peasants, more than 20,000,000. About a million of them were serfs, the rest were free men, yet their lot was an unhappy one. The burdens of society fell with crushing weight upon them. They paid fifty-five per cent of what they were able to earn to the state, according to the sober estimate of Turgot. They paid tithes to the clergy and numerous and vexatious feudal dues to the nobles. The peasant paid tolls to the seignior for the use of the roads and bridges. When he sold his land he paid a fee to the former seignior. He was compelled to use the soigneur's winepress in making his wine, the soigneur's mill, the soigneur's oven, always paying for the service. The loss of money was one aspect of the business, the loss of time another. In some cases, for instance, the mill was four or five hours distant, and a dozen or more rivers and rivulets had to be crossed. In summer, even if the water was too low to turn the wheel, nevertheless the peasant was obliged to bring his grain to be ground, must wait perhaps three days or must pay a fee for permission to have the grain ground elsewhere. Adding what he paid to the king, the church, and the seignior, and the salt and excise duties, the total was often not far from four-fifths of his earnings. With the remaining one-fifth he had to support himself and family.

The inevitable consequence was that he lived on the verge of disaster. Bad weather at a critical moment supervening, he faced dire want, even starvation. It happened that the harvest was bad in 1788 and that the following winter was cruelly severe. According to a foreign ambassador water froze almost in front of the fireplace. It need occasion no surprise that owing to such conditions hundreds of thousands of men became beggars or brigands, driven to frenzy by hunger. It has been estimated that in Paris alone, with a population of 650,000, there were nearly 120,000 paupers. No wonder there were abundant recruits for riots and deeds of violence. The 20,000,000 peasants, who knew nothing of statecraft, who were ignorant of the destructive and subversive theories of Voltaire and Rousseau, were daily and hourly impressed with the imperative necessity of reforms by the hard circumstances of their lives. They knew that the feudal dues would have to be abolished, that the excessive exactions of the state would have to be reduced before their lives could become tolerable. Their reasons for desiring change were different from those of the other classes, but it is evident that they were more than sufficient.

The combined demand for reform increased as time went on and swelled in volume and in intensity. The voice of the people spoke with no uncertain sound.

Such was the situation. On the eve of the Revolution Frenchmen enjoyed no equality of status or opportunity, but privileges of the most varied kinds divided them from each other.

They also enjoyed no liberty. Religious liberty was lacking. Since the revocation of the Edict of Nantes in 1685 Protestantism had been outlawed. It was a crime punishable with hard labor to practise that religion. Under Louis XVI the persecution of Protestants was in fact suspended, but it might be resumed at any moment. Protestant preaching was forbidden and consequently could occur only in secret or in lonely places. Jews were considered foreigners and as such were tolerated, but their position was humiliating. Catholics were required by law to observe the requirements and usages of their religion, communion, fast days, Lent. The church was absolutely opposed to toleration and because of this incurred the animosity of Voltaire.

There was no liberty of thought or, at least, of the expression of it. Every book, every newspaper article must be submitted to the censor for approval before publication, and no printer might print without permission. Even when published in conformity with these conditions books might be seized and burned by the police, editions destroyed when possible, and publishers, authors, readers might be prosecuted and fined or imprisoned. Let no one think that the mere fact that Rousseau, Voltaire, and the other authors of the day were able to get their thoughts before the public proves that liberty really existed in practice, even if not in theory. Voltaire was imprisoned several times for what he wrote and was virtually exiled during long years of his life. The censorship was applied capriciously, but it was applied sufficiently often and prosecutions were sufficiently numerous, to justify the statement that liberty was lacking in this sphere of life.

There was no individual liberty. The authorities might arrest anyone whom they wished and keep him in prison as long as they chose without assigning reasons and without giving the victim any chance to prove his innocence. There was no such thing as a Habeas Corpus law. There was a large number of state prisons, the most famous being the Bastille, and many of their occupants were there by reason of the lettres de cachet, or orders for arbitrary arrest, one of the most odious and hated features of the Old Regime. Ministers and their subordinate officials used these letters freely. Nobles easily obtained them, sometimes the place for the name being left blank for them to fill in. Sometimes, even, they were sold. Thus there was abundant opportunity to use them to pay off merely personal grudges. Malesherbes once said to Louis XVI, "No citizen of your realm is sure of not seeing his liberty sacrificed to private spite, the spirit of revenge: for no one is so great as to be safe from the hatred of a minister, so little as to be unworthy of that of a clerk." Lettres de cachet were also used as a measure of family discipline, to buttress the authority of the head of the family, which was quite as absolute as it is in the Orient. A father could have his wife imprisoned or his children, even though they were adults. Mirabeau had this experience even when he was already widely known as a writer on public affairs.

Nor was there political liberty. The French did not have the right to hold public meetings or to form associations or societies. And of course, as we have seen, they did not elect any assemblies to control the royal government. Liberties which had been in vogue in England for centuries, which were the priceless heritage of the English race on both sides of the Atlantic, were unknown in France.

In view of all these facts it is not strange that Liberty and Equality became the battle cry of the Revolution, embodying the deepest aspirations of the nation.

The French Revolution has been frequently ascribed to the influence of the "philosophers" or writers of the eighteenth century. This is putting the cart before the horse, not the usual or efficient way of insuring progress. The manifold ills from which the nation suffered only too palpably were the primary cause of the demand for a cure.

Nevertheless it was a fact of great importance that all the conditions described above, and many others, were criticised through the century by a group of brilliant writers, whose exposition and denunciation gave vocal expression on a vast scale to the discontent, the indignation, and the longing of the age. Literature was a lusty and passionate champion of reform, and through it a flood of new ideas swept over France. Many of these ideas were of foreign origin, German, American, above all English; many were of native growth. Literature was political, and never was there such a raking criticism, from every angle, of prevalent ideas. It was skeptical and expressed the greatest contempt for the traditional — that is, for the very basis on which France uneasily rested. It was analytical, and ideas and institutions and methods were subjected to the most minute and exhaustive examination. No cranny of sequestered abuse or folly was left unexplored by these eager and inquisitive and irreverent minds, on whom the past hung lightly. Literature was optimistic, and never did a nation witness so luxuriant or tropical a growth of Utopias and dreams. Rarely has anybody of writing been so charged and surcharged with freshness and boldness and reckless confidence. Appealing to reason, appealing to the emotions, it ran up and down the gamut of human nature, playing with ease and fervor upon the minds and hearts of men, in every tone, with every accent. It was a literature of criticism, of denunciation, of ingenious or futile suggestions for a fairer future. Sparkling, vehement, satirical, scientific in form, it breathed revolt, detestation, but it breathed also an abounding faith in the infinite perfectibility of man and his institutions. It was destructive, as has often been said. It was constructive, too, a characteristic which has not so often been noted. These books, which issued in great profusion from the facile pens and teeming brains of Montesquieu, Voltaire, Rousseau, Diderot, Quesnay, and many others, stirred the intellectual world to its depths. They accelerated the circulation of multifarious ideas on politics, religion, society, business. They constituted great historic acts. They crystallized in brilliant and sometimes blinding formulas and theorems whole philosophies of the state and of society. In such compact and manageable form they made the tour of France and began the tour of Europe.

The volume of this inflammable literature was large, its impetus tremendous. It exhaled the love of liberty, the craving for justice. Liberal ideas penetrated more and more deeply into the public mind. A vast fermentation, an incessant and fearless discussion of existing evils and their remedies prepared the way for coming events which were to prove of momentous character.

For three generations the fire of criticism and satire rained upon the foundations of the French monarchy. The campaign was opened by Montesquieu, a member of the nobility of the robe, a lawyer of eminence, a judge of the Parliament of Bordeaux. His great work, the product of twenty years of labor, was his Spirit of Laws, published in 1748. It had an immediate and immense success. Twenty-two editions issued from the press in eighteen months. It was a study in political philosophy, an analysis of the various forms of government known to men, a cold and balanced judgment of their various peculiarities, merits, and defects. Tearing aside the veil of mystery which men had thrown about their institutions, disregarding contemptuously the claim of a divine origin, of a sacrosanct and inviolable quality inherent in their very nature, Montesquieu examined the various types with the same detachment and objectivity which a botanist shows in the study of his specimens. Two or three leading ideas emerged from the process. One was that the English government was on the whole the best, since it guaranteed personal liberty to all citizens. It was a monarchy which was limited in power, and controlled by an assembly which represented the people of England — in other words what, in the language of modern political science, is called a constitutional monarchy. Montesquieu also emphasized the necessity in any well-regulated state of separating carefully the three powers of government, the legislative, the executive, and the judicial. In the French monarchy all were blended and fused in the single person of the king, and were subject to no earthly control — and, as a matter of fact, to no divine control that was perceptible. These conceptions of a constitutional as preferable to an absolute monarchy, and of the necessity of providing for a separation of the three powers, have dominated all the constitutions France has had since 1789 and have exerted an influence far beyond the boundaries of that country. Propounded by a studious judge, in language that was both grave and elegant, Montesquieu's masterpiece was a storehouse of wisdom, destined to be provocative of much thought, discussion, and action, both in France and elsewhere.

Very different, but even more memorable, was the work of Voltaire, one of the master minds of European history, whose name has become the name of an era. We speak of the age of Voltaire as we speak of the age of Luther and of Erasmus. Voltaire stands for the emancipation of the intellect. His significance to his times is shown in the title men gave him — King Voltaire. The world has not often seen a freer or more intrepid spirit. Supremely gifted for a life of letters, Voltaire proved himself an accomplished poet, historian, dramatist, even scientist, for he was not a specialist, but versatility was his forte. Well known at the age of twenty-three, he died at the age of eighty-four in a veritable delirium of applause, for his exit from the world was an amazing apotheosis. World-renowned he melted into world history.

He had not trod the primrose path of dalliance but had been a warrior all his life for multifarious and generally honorable causes. With many weaknesses of character, of which excessive vanity was one, he was a pillar of cloud by day and of fire by night for all who enlisted in the fight for the liberation of mankind. He had personally experienced the oppression of the Old Regime and he hated it with a deep and abiding hatred. He had several times been thrown into prison by the odious arbitrary lettres de cachet because he had incurred the enmity of the great. A large part of his life had been spent in exile because he was not safe in France. By his prodigious intellectual activity he had amassed a large fortune and had become one of the powers of Europe. Show him a case of arbitrary injustice, a case of religious persecution hounding an innocent man to an awful death — and there were such cases — and you would see him taking the field, aflame with wrath against the authors of the monstrous deed. It was literally true in the age of Voltaire that the pen was far mightier than the sword. His style has been superlatively praised and cannot be praised too highly. Clear, pointed, supple, trenchant, it was a Damascus blade. He was never tiresome, he was always interesting, and he was generally instructive. The buoyancy of his spirit was shown in everything he wrote. A master of biting satire and of pulverizing invective, he singled out particularly for his attention the hypocrisies and cruelties and bigotries of his age and he raked them with a rapid and devastating fire. This brought him into conflict with the state and the church. He denounced the abuses and iniquities of the laws and the judicial system, of arbitrary imprisonment, of torture. Voltaire was not a careful and sober student, like Montesquieu. In an age which had no journalism he was the most brilliant and mordant of journalists, writing as he listed, on the events or problems of his day. The variety and piquancy of his writings were astonishing.

Voltaire was not primarily a political thinker. He attacked individual abuses in the state and he undermined the respect for authority, but he evidently was satisfied with monarchy as an institution. His ideal of government was a benevolent despotism. He was not a democrat. He would rather be ruled by one lion than by a hundred rats, was the way in which he expressed his preference.

The church was his bete noire, as he considered it the gloomy fastness of moldering superstitions, the enemy of freedom of thought, the persecutor of innocent men who differed from it, as the seat of intolerance, as the supporter of all kinds of narrow and bigoted prejudices. Voltaire was not an atheist. He believed in God, but he did not believe in the Christian or in the Hebrew God, and he hated the Roman Catholic Church and all its works and dealt it many redoubtable blows. In eighteenth-century France the church, as we have seen, presented plenty of vulnerable sides for his fiery shafts. Voltaire's work was not constructive but destructive. His religious faith was vague at best and not very vital. He scorned all formal creeds.

Very different in tone and tendency was the work of another author, Jean Jacques Rousseau. In Voltaire we have the dry, white light of reason thrown upon the dark places of the world. In Rousseau we have reason, or rather logic, suffused and powerfully refracted with emotion. If the former was primarily engaged in the attempt to destroy, the latter was constructive, imaginative, prophetic. Rousseau was the creator of an entire political system, he was the confident theorist of a new organization of society. Montesquieu and Voltaire desired political reforms in the interest of individual liberty, desired the end of tyranny. But Rousseau swept far beyond them, wishing a total reorganization of society, because no amount of patching and renovating could make the present system tolerable, because nothing less would render liberty possible. He wrote a magic prose, rich, sonorous, full of melancholy, full of color, of musical cadences, of solemn and pensive eloquence. The past had no power over him; he lacked completely the historical sense. The past, indeed, he despised. It was to him the enemy par excellence, the cause of all the multiplied ills from which humanity was suffering and must free itself. Angry with the world as it was — his own life had been hard — he, the son of a Genevan watchmaker, had wandered here and there practising different trades, valet, music-teacher, tutor — he had known misery and had no personal reason for thinking well of the world and its boasted civilization. In his first work he propounded his fundamental thesis that man, naturally good and just and happy, had been corrupted and degraded by the very thing he called civilization. Therefore sweep civilization aside, and on the ground freed from its artificial and baneful conventions and institutions erect the idyllic state.

Rousseau's principal work was his Social Contract, one of the most famous and in its results one of the most influential books ever written. Opening with the startling statement that "man was born free and is everywhere in chains," he proceeded to outline, by pure abstract reasoning, and with a lofty disregard of all that history had to teach and all that psychology revealed of the nature of the human mind, a purely ideal state, which was in complete contrast to the one in which he lived. Society rests only upon an agreement of the persons who compose it. The people are sovereign, not any individual, nor any class. All men are free and equal. The purpose of any government should be to preserve the rights of each. Rousseau did not at all agree with Montesquieu, whose praise of the English form of government as insuring personal liberty he considered fallacious. "The English think themselves free," he said, "but they are mistaken, for they are free only at the moment in which they elect the members of Parliament." As soon as these are chosen, the people are slaves, they are nothing, since the members of Parliament are rulers, not the people. Only when the next election comes round will they be free again, and then only for another moment. Rousseau repudiated the representative system of government and demanded that the people make the laws themselves directly. Government must be government by majorities. The majority may make mistakes, nevertheless it is always right, — a dark saying. Rousseau's state made no provision for safeguarding any rights of the minority which the majority might wish to infringe. The harmful feature of his system was that it rendered possible a tyranny by a majority over a minority quite as complete and odious and unrestrained as any tyranny of a king could be. But two of his ideas stood out in high relief — the sovereignty of the people and the political equality of all citizens, two democratic principles which were utterly subversive of the states of Europe as then constituted. These principles powerfully influenced the course of the Revolution and have been preached with fervor and denounced with passion by rival camps ever since. They have made notable progress in the world since Rousseau gave them thrilling utterance, but they have still much ground to traverse before they gain the field, before the reign of democracy everywhere prevails.

There were many other writers who, by attacking this abuse and that, contributed powerfully to the discrediting, the sapping of the Old Regime. A conspicuous group of them busied themselves with economic studies and theories, enunciating principles which, if applied, would revolutionize the industrial and commercial life of the nation by sweeping away the numerous and formidable restrictions which hampered it and which permeated it with favoritism and privilege, and by introducing the maximum of liberty in commerce, in industry, in agriculture, just as the writers whom we have described enunciated principles which would revolutionize France politically and socially.

All this seed fell upon fruitful soil. Remarkable was to be the harvest, as we shall shortly see.

The Revolution was not caused by the philosophers, but by the conditions and evils of the national life and by the mistakes of the government. Nevertheless these writers were a factor in the Revolution, for they educated a group of leaders, instilled into them certain decisive doctrines, furnished them with phrases, formulas, and arguments, gave a certain tone and cast to their minds, imparted to them certain powerful illusions, encouraged an excessive hopefulness which was characteristic of the movement. They did not cause the Revolution, but they exposed the causes brilliantly, focussed attention upon them, compelled discussion, and aroused passion.

# CHAPTER II

## BEGINNINGS OF THE REVOLUTION

UNDER Louis XVI the financial situation of the country became more and more serious, until it could no longer be ignored. The cost of the participation in the American Revolution, added to the enormous debt inherited from the reigns of Louis XIV and Louis XV and to the excessive and unregulated expenditures of the state and the wastefulness of the court, completed the derangement of the national finances and foreshadowed bankruptcy. In the end this crisis forced the monarch to make an appeal to the people by summoning their representatives.

But before taking so grave a step, the consequences of which were incalculable, the government tried various expedients less drastic, which, however, for various reasons, failed. Louis XVI was the unhappy monarch under whom these long accumulating ills culminated. The last of the rulers of the Old Regime, his reign covered the years from 1774 to 1792. It falls into three periods, a brief one of attempted reform (1774-1776) and then a relapse for the next twelve years into the traditional methods of the Bourbon monarchy, after that the hurricane.

During his youth no one thought that Louis would ever be monarch, so many other princes stood between him and the throne that his succession was only a remote contingency. But owing to an unprecedented number of deaths in the direct line this contingency became reality. Louis mounted the throne, from which eighteen years later, by a strange concourse of events, he was hurled. He had never been molded for the high and dangerous office. He was but twenty years old and the Queen, Marie Antoinette, but nineteen when they heard of the death of Louis XV, and instinctively both expressed the same thought, "How unhappy are we. We are too young to rule." The new king was entirely untrained in the arts of government. He was good, well-intentioned, he had a high standard of morality and duty, a genuine desire to serve his people. But his mind lacked all distinction, his education had been poor, his processes of thought were hesitating, slow, uncertain. Awkward, timid, without elegancies or graces of mind or body, no king could have been less to the manner born, none could have seemed more out of place in the brilliant, polished, and heartless court of which he was the center. This he felt himself, as others felt it, and he often regretted, even before the Revolution, that he could not abdicate and pass into a private station which would have been far more to his taste. He was an excellent horseman, he was excessively fond of hunting, he practised with delight the craft of locksmith. He was ready to listen to the advice of wiser men, but, and this was his fatal defect, he was of feeble will. He had none of the masterful qualities necessary for leadership. He was quite unable to see where danger lay and where support was to be found. He was not unintelligent, but his intelligence was unequal to his task. He had no clear conception of either France or Europe. He was a poor judge of men, yet was greatly influenced by them. He gave way now to this influence, which might be good, now to that, which might be bad. He was, by nature, like other princes of his time, a reforming monarch, but his impulses in this direction were intermittent. Necker said on one occasion, "You may lend a man your ideas, you cannot lend him your strength of will." "Imagine," said another, "trying to keep a dozen oiled ivory balls touching. I think you couldn't do it." So it was with the King's ideas. At the beginning of his reign Louis XVI was subject to the influence of Turgot, one of the wisest of statesmen. Later he was subject to the influence of the Queen — to his own great misfortune and also to that of France.

The influence of women was always great in France under the Bourbon monarchy, and Marie Antoinette was no exception to the rule. Furthermore that influence was frequently disastrous, and here again in the case of the last queen of the Old Regime there was no exception. If the King proved inferior to his position, the Queen proved no less inferior to hers. She was the daughter of the great Empress Maria Theresa of Austria, and she had been married to Louis XVI in the hope that thus an alliance would be cemented between the two states which had so long been enemies. But, as many Frenchmen disliked everything about this alliance, she was unpopular and exposed to much malevolent criticism from the moment she set foot in France. She was beautiful, gracious, and vivacious. She possessed in large measure some of the very qualities the King so conspicuously lacked. She had a strong will, power of rapid decision, a spirit of initiative, daring. But she was lacking in wisdom, in breadth of judgment; she did not understand the temperament of the French people nor the spirit of the times. Born to the purple, her outlook upon life did not transcend that of the small and highly privileged class to which she belonged.

She had grown up in Vienna, one of the gayest capitals of Europe. Her education was woefully defective. When she came to France to become the wife of Louis XVI, she hardly knew how to write. She had had tutors in everything, but they had availed her little. She was wilful and proud, unthinking and extravagant, intolerant of disagreeable facts, frivolous, impatient of all restraint, fond of pleasure and of those who ministered unto it. She committed many indiscretions both in her conduct and in the kind of people she chose to have about her. Because of these she was grossly calumniated and misjudged.

Marie Antoinette was the center of a group of rapacious people who benefited by existing abuses, who were opposed to all reform. Quite unconsciously she helped to aggravate the financial situation and thus to hasten catastrophe.

At the beginning of his reign Louis intrusted the management of finances to a man of rare ability and courage, Turgot. Turgot had been intendant of one of the poorest provinces of France. By applying there the principles of the most advanced economists, which may be summed up as demanding the utmost liberty for industry and trade, the abolition of all artificial restrictions and all minute and vexatious governmental regulations, he had made his province prosperous. He now had to face the problem of the large annual deficit. The continuance of annual deficits could mean nothing else than ultimate bankruptcy. Turgot announced his program to the King in the words, "No bankruptcy, no increase of taxation, no more borrowing." He hoped to extricate the national finances by two processes, by effecting economies in expenditures, and by developing public wealth so that the receipts would be larger. The latter object would be achieved by introducing the regime of liberty into agriculture, industry, and commerce. Turgot was easily able to save many millions by suppressing useless expenditures, but in so doing he offended all who enjoyed those sinecures, and they flew to arms. The trade in foodstuffs was hopelessly and dangerously hampered by all sorts of artificial and pernicious legislation and interference by the state. All this he swept aside, introducing free trade in grain. A powerful class of speculators was thus offended. He abolished the trade guilds, which restricted production by limiting the number of workers in each line, and by guarding jealously the narrow, inelastic monopolies they had established. Their abolition was desirable, but all the masters of the guilds and corporations became his bitter enemies. Turgot abolished an odious tax, the royal corvee, which required the peasants to work without pay on the public roads. Instead, he provided that all such work should be paid for and that a tax to that end should be levied upon all landowners, whether belonging to the privileged or the unprivileged classes. The former were resolved that this should not be, this odious equality of all before the tax-collector. Thus all those who battened and fattened off the old system combined in merciless opposition to Turgot and, reinforced by the parlements particularly, and by Marie Antoinette, they brought great pressure upon the King to dismiss the obnoxious minister. Louis yielded to the vehement importunities of the Queen and dismissed the ablest supporter the throne had. In this both monarchs were grievously at fault, the King for his lack of will, the Queen for her wilfulness. "M. Turgot and I are the only persons who love the people," said Louis XVI, but he did not prove his love by his acts. A few days earlier Turgot had written him, "Never forget, your Majesty, that it was weakness which brought Charles I to the block."

This incident threw a flood of light upon the nature of the Old Regime. All reformers were given warning by the fall of Turgot. No changes that should affect the privileged classes! As the national finances could be made sound only by reforms which should affect those classes, there was no way out. Reform was blocked. Necker, a Genevan banker, succeeded Turgot. He was a man who had risen by his own efforts from poverty to great wealth. He, too, encountered opposition the instant he proposed economies. He took a step which infuriated the members of the court. He published a financial report, showing the income and the expenditures of the state. This had never been done before, secrecy having hitherto prevailed in such matters. The court was indignant that such high mysteries should be revealed to the masses, particularly as the report showed just how much went annually in pensions to the courtiers, as free gifts for which they rendered no services whatever. For such unconscionable audacity Necker was overthrown, the King weakly yielding once more to pressure.

This time the court took no chances, but secured a minister quite according to the heart's desire, in Calonne. No minister of finance could be more agreeable. Calonne's purpose was to please, and please he did, for a while. The wand of Prospero was not more felicitous in its enchantments. The members of the court had only to make their wishes known to have them gratified.

Calonne, a man of charm, of wit, of graceful address, had also a philosophy of the gentle art of spending which was highly appreciated by those about him. "A man who wishes to borrow must appear to be rich, and to appear rich he must dazzle by spending freely." Money flowed like water during these halcyon times. In three years, in a time of profound peace, Calonne borrowed nearly $300,000,000.

It seemed too good to be true, and it was, by far. The evil days drew nigh for an accounting. It was found in August, 1786, that the treasury was empty and that there were no more fools willing to loan to the state. It was a rude awakening from a blissful dream. But Calonne now showed, what he had not shown before, some sense. He proposed a general tax which should fall upon the nobles as well as upon commoners. It was therefore his turn to meet the same opposition from the privileged classes which Turgot and Necker had met. He, too, was balked, and resigned.

His successor, Lomenie de Brienne, encountered a similar fate. As there was nothing to do but to propose new taxes, he proposed them. The Parliament of Paris immediately protested and demanded the convocation of the States-General, asserting the far-reaching principle that taxes can only be imposed by those who are to pay them. The King attempted to overawe the parliament, which, in turn, defied the King. All this, however, was no way to fill an empty treasury. Finally the government yielded and summoned the States-General to meet in Versailles on May 1, 1789. A new chapter, of incalculable possibilities, was opened in the history of France. Necker was recalled to head the ministry, and preparations for the coming meeting were made.

The States-General, or assembly representing the three estates of the realm, the clergy, the nobility, and the commoners, was an old institution in France, but one that had never developed as had the parliament of England. The last meeting, indeed, had been held 175 years before. The institution might have been considered dead. Now, in a great national crisis, it was revived, in the hope that it might pull the state out of the deplorable situation into which the Bourbon monarchy had plunged it. But the States-General was a thoroughly feudal institution and France was tired of feudalism. Its organization no longer conformed to the wishes or needs of the nation.

Previously each one of the three estates had had an equal number of delegates, and the delegates of each estate had met separately. It was a three-chambered body, with two of the chambers consisting entirely of the privileged classes. There was objection to this now, since, with two against one, it left the nation exactly where it had been, in the power of the privileged classes. They could veto anything that the third estate alone wanted; they could impose anything they chose upon the third estate, by their vote of two to one. In other words, if organized as hitherto, they could prevent all reform which in any way affected themselves, and yet such reform was an absolute necessity. Consulted on this problem the Parliament of Paris pronounced in favor of the customary organization; in other words, itself a privileged body, it stood for privilege. The parliament immediately became as unpopular as it had previously been popular, when opposing the monarch.

Necker, now showing one of his chief characteristics which was to make him impossible as a leader in the new era, half settled the question and left it half unsettled. He, like the King, lacked the power of decision. He was a banker, not a statesman. It was announced that the third estate should have as many members as the two other orders combined. Whether the three bodies should still meet and vote separately was not decided, but was left undetermined. But of what avail would be the double membership of the third estate — representing more than nine-tenths of the population — unless all three met together, unless the vote was by individuals, not by chambers; by head, as the phrase ran, and not by order? In dodging this question Necker was merely showing his own incapacity for strong leadership and was laying up abundant trouble for the immediate future.

The States-General met on May 5, 1789. There were about 1,200 members, of whom over 600 were members of the third estate. In reality, however, that class of the population had a much larger representation, as, of the 300 representatives elected by the clergy, over 200 were parish priests or monks, all commoners by origin and, to a considerable extent, in sympathy. Each of the three orders had elected its own members. At the same time the voters, and the vote was nearly universal, were asked to draw up a formal statement of their grievances and of the reforms they favored. Fifty or sixty thousand of these cahiers have come down to us and present a vivid and instructive criticism of the Old Regime, and a statement of the wishes of each order. On certain points there was practical unanimity on the part of clergy, nobles, and commoners. All ascribed the ills from which the country suffered to arbitrary, uncontrolled government, all talked of the necessity of confining the government within just limits by establishing a constitution which should define the rights of the king and of the people, and which should henceforth be binding upon all. Such a constitution must guarantee individual liberty, the right to think and speak and write, — henceforth no lettres de cachet nor censorship. In the future the States-General should meet regularly at stated times, and should share the law-making power and alone should vote the taxes, and taxes should henceforth be paid by all. The clergy and nobility almost unanimously agreed in their cahiers to relinquish their exemptions, for which they had fought so resolutely only two years before. On the other hand, the third estate was willing to see the continuance of the nobility with its rights and honors. The third estate demanded the suppression of feudal dues. There was in their cahiers no hint of a desire for a violent revolution. They all expressed a deep affection for the King, gratitude for his summoning of the States-General, faith that the worst was over, that now, in a union of all hearts, a way would easily be discovered out of the unhappy plight in which the nation found itself.

An immense wave of hopefulness swept over the land. This optimism was based on the fact that the King, when consenting to call the States-General, had at the same time announced his acceptance of several important reforms, such as the periodical meeting of the States-General, its control of the national finances, and guarantees for the freedom of the individual. But the King's chief characteristic, as we have seen, was his feebleness of will, his vacillation. And from the day the deputies arrived in Versailles to the day of his violent overthrow this was a fatal factor in the history of the times. In his speech opening the States-General on May 5 the King said not a word about the thought that was in every one's mind, the making of a constitution. He merely announced that it had been called together to bring order into the distracted finances of the country. Necker's speech was no more promising. The government, moreover, said nothing about whether the estates should vote by order or by head. The crux of the whole matter lay there, for on the manner of organization and procedure depended entirely the outcome. The government did not come forward with any program, even in details. It shirked its responsibility and lost its opportunity.

A needless but very serious crisis was the result. The public was disappointed and apprehensive. Evidently the recent liberalism of the King had evaporated or he was under a pressure which he had not strength to withstand. A conflict between the orders began on May 6 which lasted until the end of June and which ended in embittering relations which at the outset had seemed likely to be cordial. Should the voting be by order or by member, should the assembly consist of three chambers or of one? The difficulty arose in the need of verifying the credentials of the members. The nobles proceeded to verify as a separate chamber, by a vote of 188 to 47; the clergy did the same, but by a smaller majority, 133 to 114. But the third estate refused to verify until it should be decided that the three orders were to meet together in one indivisible assembly. This was a matter of life or death with it, or at least of power or impotence. Both sides stood firm, the government allowed things to drift, angry passions began to develop. Until organized the States-General could do no business, and no organization could be effected until this crucial question was settled. Week after week went by and the dangerous deadlock continued. Verification in common would mean the abandonment of the class system, voting by member and not by order, and the consequent preponderance of the third estate, which considered that it had the right to preponderate as representing over nine-tenths of the population. Fruitless attempts to win the two upper orders by inviting them to join the third estate were repeatedly made. Finally the third estate announced that on June n it would begin verification and the other orders were invited for the last time. Then the parish priests began to come over, sympathizing with the commoners rather than with the privileged class of their own order. Finally on June 17 the third estate took the momentous step of declaring itself the National Assembly, a distinctly revolutionary proceeding.

The King now, under pressure from the court, made a decision, highly unwise in itself and foolishly executed. When, on June 20, the members of the third estate went to their usual meeting-place they found the entrance blocked by soldiers. They were told that there was to be a special royal session later and that the hall was closed in order that necessary arrangements might be made for it, a pretext as miserable as it was vain. What did this action mean? No one knew, but everyone was apprehensive that it meant that the Assembly itself, in which such earnest hopes had centered, was to be brought to an untimely end and the country plunged into greater misery than ever by the failure of the great experiment. For a moment the members were dismayed and utterly distracted. Then, as by a common impulse, they rushed to a neighboring building in a side street, which served as a tennis court. There a memorable session occurred, in the large, unfinished hall. Lifting their president, the distinguished astronomer, Bailly, to a table, the members surged about him, ready, it seemed, for extreme measures. There they took the famous Tennis Court Oath. All the deputies present, with one single exception, voted "never to separate, and to reassemble wherever circumstances shall require, until the constitution of the kingdom shall be established."

On the 23rd occurred the royal session on which the privileged classes counted. The King pronounced the recent acts of the third estate illegal and unconstitutional, and declared that the three orders should meet separately and verify their credentials. He rose and left the hall, while outside the bugles sounded around his coach. The nobility, triumphant, withdrew from the hall; the clergy also. But in the center of the great chamber the third estate remained, in gloomy silence. This was one of the solemn, critical moments of history. Suddenly the master of ceremonies advanced, resplendent in his official costume. "You have heard the King's orders," he said. "His Majesty requests the deputies of the third estate to withdraw." Behind the grand master, at the door, soldiers were seen. Were they there to clear the hall? The King had given his orders. To leave the hall meant abandonment of all that the third estate stood for; to remain meant disobedience to the express commands of the King and probably severe punishment.

The occasion brought forth its man. Mirabeau, a noble whom his fellow nobles had refused to elect to the States-General and who had then been chosen by the third estate, now arose and advanced impetuously and imperiously toward the master of ceremonies, de Breze, and with thunderous voice exclaimed, "Go tell your master that we are here by the will of the people and that we shall not leave except at the point of the bayonet." Then on motion of Mirabeau it was voted that all persons who should lay violent hands on any members of the National Assembly would be "infamous and traitors to the nation and guilty of capital crime." De Breze reported the defiant eloquence to the King. All eyes were fixed upon the latter. Not knowing what to do he made a motion indicating weariness, then said: "They wish to remain, do they? Well, let them."

Two days later a majority of the clergy and a minority of the nobility came over to the Assembly. On June 27 the King commanded the nobility and clergy to sit with the third estate in a single assembly. Thus the question was finally settled, which should have been settled before the first meeting in May. The National Assembly was now complete. It immediately appointed a committee on the constitution. The National Assembly, accomplished by this fusion of the three estates, adopted the title Constituent Assembly because of the character of the work it had to do.

No sooner was this crisis over than another began to develop. A second attempt was made by the King, again inspired by the court, to suppress the Assembly or effectively to intimidate it, to regain the ground that had been lost. Considerable bodies of soldiers began to appear near Versailles and Paris. They were chiefly the foreign mercenaries, or the troops from frontier stations, supposedly less responsive to the popular emotions. On July n Necker and his colleagues, favorable to reform, were suddenly dismissed and Necker was ordered to leave the country immediately. What could all this mean but that reaction and repression were coming and that things were to be put back where they had been? The Assembly was in great danger, yet it possessed no physical force. What could it do if troops were sent against it?

The violent intervention of the city of Paris saved the day and gave the protection which the nation's representatives lacked, assuring their continuance. The storming of the Bastille was an incident which seized instantly the imagination of the world, and which was disfigured and transfigured by a mass of legends that sprang up on the very morrow of the event. The Bastille was a fortress commanding the eastern section of Paris. It was used as a state prison and had had many distinguished occupants, among others Voltaire and Mirabeau, thrown into it by lettres de cachet. It was an odious symbol of arbitrary government and it was also a strong fortress which these newly arriving troops might use. There was a large discontented and miserable class in Paris; also a lively band of radical or liberal men who were in favor of reform and were alarmed and indignant at every rumor that the Assembly on which such hopes were pinned was in danger. Paris was on the side of the Assembly, and when the news of the dismissal of Necker arrived it took fire. Rumors of the most alarming character spread rapidly. Popular meetings were addressed by impromptu and impassioned orators. The people began to pillage the shops where arms were to be found. Finally they attacked the Bastille and after a confused and bloody battle of several hours the fortress was in their hands. They had lost about 200 men, killed or wounded. The crowd savagely murdered the commander of the fortress and several of the Swiss Guard. Though characterized by these and other acts of barbarism, nevertheless the seizure of the Bastille was everywhere regarded in France and abroad as the triumph of liberty. Enthusiasm was widespread. The Fourteenth of July was declared the national holiday and a new flag, the tricolor, the red, white, and blue, was adopted in place of the old white banner of the Bourbons, studded with the fleur-de-lis. At the same time, quite spontaneously, Paris gave itself a new form of municipal government, superseding the old royal form, and organized a new military force, the National Guard, which was destined to become famous. Three days later Louis XVI came to the capital and formally ratified these changes.

Meanwhile similar changes were made all over France. Municipal governments on an elective basis and national guards were created everywhere in imitation of Paris. The movement extended to rural France. There the peasants, impatient that the Assembly had let two months go by without suppressing the feudal dues, took things into their own hands. They turned upon their oppressors and made a violent "war upon the chateaux," destroying the records of feudal dues if they could find them or if the owners gave them up; if not, frequently burning the chateaux themselves in order to burn the odious documents. Day after day in the closing week of July, 1789, the destructive and incendiary process went on amid inevitable excesses and disorders. In this method feudalism was abolished — not legally but practically. It remained to be seen what the effect of this victory of the people would be upon the National Assembly.

Its effect was immediate and sensational. On the 4th of August a committee on the state of the nation made a report, describing the incidents which were occurring throughout the length and breadth of the land, chateaux burning, unpopular tax-collectors assaulted, millers hanged, lawlessness triumphant. It was night before the stupefying report was finished. Suddenly at eight o'clock in the evening, as the session was about to close, a nobleman, the Viscount of Noailles, rushed to the platform. The only reason, he said, why the people had devastated the chateaux was the heavy burden of the seigniorial dues, odious reminders of feudalism. These must be swept away. He so moved and instantly another noble, the Duke d'Aiguillon, next to the King the greatest feudal lord in France, seconded the motion. A frenzy of generosity seized the Assembly. Noble vied with noble in the enthusiasm of renunciation. The Bishop of Nancy renounced the privileges of his order. Parish priests renounced their fees. Judges discarded their distinctions. Rights of chase, rights of tithes went by the board. Representatives of the cities and provinces gave up their privileges, Brittany, Burgundy, Lorraine, Languedoc. A veritable delirium of joy swept in wave after wave over the Assembly. All night long the excitement continued amid tears, embraces, rapturous applause, a very ecstasy of patriotic abandonment, and by eight in the morning thirty decrees, more or less, had been passed and the most extraordinary social revolution that any nation has known had been voted. The feudal dues were dead. Tithes were abandoned; the guilds, with their narrow restrictions, were swept away; no longer were offices to be purchasable, but henceforth all Frenchmen were to be equally eligible to all public positions; justice was to be free; provinces and individuals were all to be on the same plane. Distinctions of class were abolished. The principle of equality was henceforth to be the basis of the state.

Years later participants in this memorable session, in which a social revolution was accomplished, or at least promised, spoke of it with excitement and enthusiasm. The astonishing session was closed with a Te Deum in the chapel of the royal palace, at the suggestion of the Archbishop of Paris, and Louis XVI, who had had no more to do with all this than you or I, was officially proclaimed by the Assembly the "Restorer of French Liberty."

Thus was the dead weight of an oppressive, unjust past lifted from the nation's shoulders. Grievances, centuries old, vanished into the night. That it needed time to work out all these tumultuous and rapturous resolutions into clear and just laws was a fact ignored by the people, who regarded them as real legislation, not as a program merely sketched, to be filled in slowly in detail. Hence when men awoke to the fact that not everything was what it seemed, that before the actual application of all these changes many adjustments must or should be made, there was some friction, some disappointment, some impatience. The clouds speedily gathered again. Because a number of nobles and bishops had in an outburst of generosity relinquished all their privileges, it was not at all certain that their action would be ratified by even the majority of their orders and it was indeed likely that the contrary would prove true. The contagion might not extend beyond the walls of the Assembly hall. And many even of those who had shared the fine enthusiasm of that stirring session might feel differently on the morrow. This proved to be the case, and soon two parties appeared, sharply differentiated, the upholders of the revolution thus far accomplished and those who wished to undo it and to recover their lost advantages. The latter were called counter-revolutionaries. From this time on they were a factor, frequently highly significant, in the history of modern France. Although after the Fourteenth of July the more stiff-necked and angry of the courtiers, led by the Count of Artois, brother of the King, had left the country and had begun that "emigration" which was to do much to embroil France with Europe, yet many courtiers still remained and, with the powerful aid of Marie Antoinette, played upon the feeble monarch. The Queen, victim of slanders and insults, was temperamentally and intellectually incapable of understanding or sympathizing with the reform movement. She stiffened under the attacks, her pride was fired, and she did what she could to turn back the tide, with results highly disastrous to herself and to the monarchy. Another feature of the situation was the subterranean intriguing, none the less real because difficult accurately to describe, of certain individuals who thought they had much to gain by troubling the waters, such as the Duke of Orleans, cousin of the King, immensely wealthy and equally unscrupulous, who nourished the scurvy ambition of overthrowing Louis XVI and of putting the House of Orleans in place of the House of Bourbon. All through the Revolution we find such elements of personal ambition or malevolence, anxious to profit by fomenting the general unrest. At every stage in this strange, eventful history we observe the mixture of the mean with the generous, the insincere with the candid, the hypocritical and the oblique with the honest and the patriotic. It was a web woven of mingled yarn.

Such were some of the possible seeds of future trouble. In addition, increasing the general sense of anxiety and insecurity, was the fact that two months went by and yet the King did not ratify or accept the decrees of August 4, which, without his acceptance, lacked legal force. Certain articles of the constitution had been already drafted, and these, too, had not yet received the royal sanction. Was the King plotting something, or were the plotters about him getting control of him once more? The people lived in an atmosphere of suspicion; also thousands and thousands of them were on the point of starvation, and the terror of famine reinforced the terror of suspicion.

Out of this wretched condition of discontent and alarm was born another of the famous incidents of the Revolution. Early in October rumors reached Paris that at a banquet offered at Versailles to some of the crack regiments that had been summoned there the tricolor had been stamped upon, that threats had been made against the Assembly, and that the Queen, by her presence, had sanctioned these outrages.

On October 5 several thousand women of the people, set in motion in some obscure way, started to march to Versailles, drawing cannon with them. It was said they were going to demand the reduction of the price of bread and at the same time to see that those who had insulted the national flag should be punished. They were followed by thousands of men, out of work, and by many doubtful characters. Lafayette, hastily gathering some of the guards, started after them. That evening the motley and sinister crowd reached Versailles and bivouacked in the streets and in the vast court of the royal palace. All night long obscure preparations as for a battle went on. On the morning of the 6th the crowd forced the gates, killed several of the guards, and invaded the palace, even reaching the entrance to the Queen's apartments. The Queen fled to the apartments of the King for safety. The King finally appeared on a balcony, surrounded by members of his family, addressed the crowd, and promised them food. The outcome of this extraordinary and humiliating day was that the King was persuaded to leave the proud palace of Versailles and go to Paris to live, in the midst of his so-called subjects. At two o'clock the grim procession began. The entire royal family, eight persons, packed into a single carriage, started for Paris, drawn at a walk, surrounded by the women, and by bandits who carried on pikes the heads of the guards who had been killed at the entrance to the palace. "We are bringing back the baker, and the baker's wife, and the baker's son!" shouted the women. At eleven o'clock that night Louis XVI was in the Tuileries.

Ten days later the Assembly followed. The King and the Assembly were now under the daily supervision of the people of Paris. In reality they were prisoners. Versailles was definitely abandoned. From this moment dates the great influence of the capital. A single city was henceforth always in position to dominate the Assembly. The people could easily bring their pressure to bear, for they were admitted to the thousand or more seats in the gallery of the Assembly's hall of meeting and they considered that they had the freedom of the place, hissing unpopular speakers, vociferating their wishes. Those who could not get in congregated outside, arguing violently the measures that were being discussed within. Now and then someone would announce to them from the windows how matters were proceeding in the hall. Shouts of approval or disapproval thus reached the members from the vehement audience outside.

# CHAPTER III

## THE MAKING OF THE CONSTITUTION

THE States-General which met in May, 1789, had in June adopted the name National Assembly. This body is also known as the Constituent Assembly, as its chief work was the making of a constitution. It had begun work upon the constitution while still in Versailles, and the first fruit of its labors was the Declaration of the Rights of Man, a statement of the rights which belong to men because they are human beings, which are not the gift of any government. The declaration was drawn up in imitation of American usage. Lafayette, a hero of the American Revolution, as now a prominent figure in the French, brought forward a draft of a declaration just before the storming of the Bastille. He urged two chief reasons for its adoption: first, it would present the people with a clear conception of the elements of liberty which, once understanding, they would insist upon possessing; and, secondly, it would be an invaluable guide for the Assembly in its work of elaborating the constitution. All propositions could be tested by comparison with its carefully defined principles. It would be a guarantee against mistakes or errors by the Assembly itself. Another orator paid a tribute to America, explaining why "the noble idea of this declaration, conceived in another hemisphere" ought to be transplanted to France. Opponents of such a statement declared it useless and harmful because bound to distract the members from important labors, as tending to waste time on doubtful generalizations, as leading to hair-splitting and endless debate, when the Assembly's attention ought to be focussed on the pressing problems of legislation and administration. The Assembly took the side of Lafayette and, after intermittent discussion, composed the notable document in August, 1789. As a result of the events of October 5, described above, the King accepted it. The declaration, which has been called "the most remarkable fact in the history of the growth of democratic and republican ideas" in France, as "the gospel of modern times," was not the work of any single mind, nor of any committee or group of leaders. Its collaborators were very numerous. The political discussions of the eighteenth century furnished many of the ideas and even some of the phrases. English and American example counted for much. The necessities of the national situation were factors of importance.

The National Assembly has often been severely criticised for devoting time, in a period of crisis, to a declaration which the critics in the same breath pronounce a tissue of abstractions, of doubtful philosophical theories, topics for ever-lasting discussion. "A tourney of metaphysical speculations" is what one writer calls it. But a study of the situation shows that the idea of a declaration and the idea of a constitution were indissolubly connected. The one was essential to the other in a country which had no historic principles of freedom. French liberty could not from the nature of the case, like English liberty, slowly broaden down from precedent to precedent. It must begin abruptly and with a distinct formulation. After the enunciation of the principles would naturally come their conversion into fact.

The Declaration of the Rights of Man laid down the principles of modern governments. The men who drew up that document believed these principles to be universally true and everywhere applicable. They did not establish rights — they merely declared them. Frenchmen well knew that they were composing a purely dogmatic text. But that such a text was extremely useful they believed. And the reason why they believed this was that they had a profound faith in the power of truth, of reason. This was, as Michelet pointed out long ago, the essential originality of the Constituent Assembly, this "singular faith in the power of ideas," this firm belief that "once formed and formulated in law the truth was invincible." These political dogmas seemed to the members of the Assembly so true that they thought they had only to proclaim them to insure their efficiency in the actual conduct of governments. These men believed that they were inaugurating a new phase in the history of humanity, that, by solemnly formulating the creed of the future, they were rendering an inestimable service, not to France alone but to the world. Though America had set an example, it was felt that France could "perfect" it for the other hemisphere and that the new declaration might perhaps have the advantage over the other of making "a loftier appeal to reason and of clothing her in a purer language."

The seventeen articles of this creed asserted that men are free and equal, that the people are sovereign, that law is an expression of the popular will, and that in the making of it the people may participate, either directly, or indirectly through their representatives, and that all officials possess only that authority which has been definitely given them by law. All those liberties of the person, of free speech, free assembly, justice administered by one's peers, which had been worked out in England and America were asserted. These principles were the opposite of those of the Old Regime. If incorporated in laws and institutions they meant the permanent abolition of that system.

As a matter of fact the expectation that the Declaration would constitute a new evangel for the world has not proved so great an exaggeration as the optimism of its authors and the pessimism of its critics would prompt one to think. When men wish anywhere to recall the rights of man it is this French document that they have in mind. The Declaration long ago passed beyond the frontiers of France. It has been studied, copied, or denounced nearly everywhere. It has been an indisputable factor in the political and social evolution of modern Europe. During the past century, whenever a nation has aspired to liberty, it has sought its principles in the Declaration. "It has found there," says a recent writer, "five or six formulas as trenchant as mathematical propositions, true as the truth itself, intoxicating as a vision of the absolute."

The Declaration was, of course, only an ideal, a goal toward which society should aim, not a fulfilment. It was a list of principles, not the realization of those principles. It was a declaration of rights, not a guarantee of rights. The problem of how to guarantee what was so succinctly declared has filled more than a century of French history, and is still incompletely solved. We shall now see how far the Assembly which drafted this Declaration was willing or able to go in applying its principles in the constitution, of which it was the preamble.

The constitution was only slowly elaborated. Some of its more fundamental articles were adopted in 1789. But numerous laws were passed in 1790 and 1791, which were really parts of the constitution. Thus it grew piece by piece. Finally all this legislation was revised, retouched, and codified into a single document, which was accepted by the King in 1791. Though sometimes called the Constitution of 1789, it is more generally and more correctly known as the Constitution of 1791. It was the first written constitution France had ever had. Framed under very different conditions from those under which the constitution of the United States had been framed only a short time before, it resembled the work of the Philadelphia Convention in that it was conspicuously the product of the spirit of compromise. With the exception of the vigorous assertions of the Declaration of the Rights of Man, the document was marked by as great a moderation as was consistent with the thoroughgoing changes that were demanded by the overwhelming public opinion, as represented in the cahiers. It is permeated through and through with two principles, the sovereignty of the people, all governmental powers issuing from their consent and will, and the separation of the powers sharply from each other, of the executive, the legislative, and the judicial branches, a division greatly emphasized by Montesquieu as the sole method of insuring liberty.

The form of government was to be monarchical. This was in conformity with the wishes of the people as expressed in the cahiers, and with the feelings of the Constituent Assembly. But whereas formerly the king was an absolute, henceforth he was to be a limited, a constitutional ruler. Indicative of the profound difference between these two conceptions, his former title, King of France and of Navarre, now gave way to that of King of the French. Whereas formerly he had taken what he chose out of the national treasury for his personal use, now he was to receive a salary or civil list of the definite amount — and no more — of 25,000,000 francs. He was to appoint the ministers or heads of the cabinet departments, but he was forbidden to select members of the legislature for such positions. The English system of parliamentary government was deliberately avoided because it was believed to be vicious in that ministers could bribe or influence the members of Parliament to do their will, which might not at all be the will of the people. Ministers were not even to be permitted to come before the legislature to defend or explain their policies.

A departure from the principle of the separation of powers, in general so closely followed, was shown in the granting of the veto power to the king. The king, who had hitherto made the laws, was now deprived of the law-making power, but he could prevent the immediate enforcement of an act passed by the legislature. There was much discussion over this subject in the Assembly. Some were opposed to any kind of a veto; others wanted one that should be absolute and final. The Assembly compromised and granted the king a suspensive veto, that is, he might prevent the application of a law voted by two successive legislatures, that is, for a possible period of four years. If the third legislature should indicate its approval of the law in question, then it was to be put into operation whether the king assented or not.

The king was to retain the conduct of foreign affairs in his own hands. He was to appoint and receive ambassadors; was to be the head of the navy and army and was to appoint to higher offices. The Assembly at first thought of leaving him the right to make peace and war, then, fearing that he might drag the nation into a war for personal or dynastic and not national purposes, it decided that he might propose peace or war, but that the legislature should decide upon it.

The legislative power was given by the Constitution of 1791 to a single assembly of 745 members, to be elected for a term of two years. Several of the deputies desired a legislature of two chambers, and cited the example of England and America. But the second chamber in England was the House of Lords, and the French, who had abolished the nobility, had no desire to establish an hereditary chamber. Moreover the English system was based on the principle of inequality. The French were founding their new system upon the principle of equality. Even among the nobles themselves there was opposition to a second chamber — the provincial nobility fearing that only the court nobles would be members of it. On the other hand, the Senate of the United States was a concession to the states-rights feeling, a feeling which the French wished to destroy by abolishing the provinces and the local provincial patriotism, by thoroughly unifying France. Thus the plan of dividing the legislature into two chambers was deliberately rejected, for what seemed good and sufficient reasons.

How was this legislature to be chosen? Here we find a decided departure from the spirit and the letter of the Declaration, which had asserted that all men are equal in rights. Did not this mean universal suffrage? Such at least was not the opinion of the Constituent Assembly, which now made a distinction between citizens, declaring some active, some passive. To be considered an active citizen one must be at least twenty-five years of age and must pay annually in direct taxes the equivalent of three days' wages. This excluded the poor from this class, and the number was large. It has been estimated that there were somewhat over 4,000,000 active citizens and about 3,000,000 passive.

The active citizens alone had the right to vote. But even they did not vote directly for the members of the legislature. They chose electors at the ratio of one for every 100 active citizens. These electors must meet a much higher property qualification, the equivalent of from 150 to 200 days' wages in direct taxes. As a matter of fact this resulted in rendering eligible as electors only about 43,000 individuals. These electors chose the members of the legislature, the deputies. They also chose the judges under the new system. Thus the Constituent Assembly, so zealous in abolishing old privileges, was, in defiance of its own principles, establishing new ones. Political rights in the new state were made the monopoly of those who possessed a certain amount of property. There was no property qualification required for deputies. Any active citizen was eligible, but as the deputies were elected by the propertied men, they would in all probability choose only propertied men — the electors would choose from their own class.

The judicial power was completely revolutionized. Hitherto judges had bought their positions, which carried with them titles and privileges and which they might pass on to their sons. Henceforth all judges, of whatever rank in the hierarchy, were to be elected by the electors described above. Their terms were to range from two to four years. The jury, something hitherto absolutely unknown to modern France, was now introduced for criminal cases. Hitherto the judge had decided all cases.

For purposes of administration and local government a new system was established. The old thirty-two provinces were abolished and France was divided into eighty-three departments of nearly uniform size. The departments were divided into arrondissements, these into cantons, and these into municipalities or communes. These are terms which have ever since been in vogue.

France, from being a highly centralized state, became one highly decentralized. Whereas formerly the central government was represented in each province by its own agents or office-holders, the intendants and their subordinates, in the departments of the future the central government was to have no representatives. The electors were to choose the local departmental officials. It would be the business of these officials to carry out the decrees of the central government but what if they should disobey? The central government would have no control over them, as it would not appoint them and could neither remove nor discipline them.

The Constitution of 1791 represented an improvement in French government; yet it did not work well and did not last long. As a first experiment in the art of self-government it had its value, but it revealed inexperience and poor judgment in several points which prepared trouble for the future. The executive and the legislature were so sharply separated that communication between them was difficult and suspicion was consequently easily fostered. The king might not select his ministers from the legislature, he might not, in case of a difference of opinion with the legislature, dissolve the latter, as the English king could do, thus allowing the voters to decide between them. The king's veto was not a weapon strong enough to protect him from the attacks of the Assembly, yet it was enough to irritate the Assembly, if used. The distinction between active and passive citizens was in plain and flagrant defiance of the Declaration of the Rights of Man, and inevitably created a discontented class. The administrative decentralization was so complete that the efficiency of the national government was gone. France was split up into eighty-three fragments, and the co-ordination of all these units, their direction toward great national ends in response to the will of the nation as a whole, was rendered extremely difficult, and in certain crises impossible. The work of reform carried out by the Constituent Assembly was on an enormous scale, immensely more extensive than that of our Federal Convention. We search history in vain for any companion piece. It is unique. Its destructive work proved durable and most important. Much of its constructive work, however, proved very fragile. Mirabeau expressed his opinion in saying that "The disorganization of the kingdom could not be better worked out."

There were other dangerous features of the situation which inspired alarm and seemed to keep open and to embitter the relations of various classes and to foster opportunities for the discontented and the ambitious. The legislation concerning the church proved highly divisive in its effects. It began with the confiscation of its property; it was continued in the attempt profoundly to alter its organization.

The States-General had been summoned to provide for the finances of the country. As the problem grew daily more pressing, as various attempts to meet it proved futile, as bankruptcy was imminent, the Assembly finally decided to sell for the state the vast properties of the church. The argument was that the church was not the owner but was merely the administrator, enjoying only the use of the vast wealth which had been bestowed upon it by the faithful, but bestowed for public, national purposes, namely, the maintenance of houses of worship, schools, hospitals; and that if the state would otherwise provide for the carrying out of the intentions of these numerous benefactors, it might apply the property, which was the property of the nation, not of the church as a corporation, to whatever uses it might see fit. Acting on this theory a decree was passed by the Assembly declaring these lands national. They constituted perhaps a fourth or a fifth of the territory of France and represented immense wealth, amply sufficient, it was believed, to set the public finances right.

But such property could only be used if converted into money and that would be a slow process, running through years. The expedient was devised of issuing paper money, as the government needed it, against this property as security. This paper money bore the name of assignats. Persons receiving such assignats could not demand gold for them, as in the case of our paper money, but could use them in buying these lands. There was value therefore behind these paper emissions. The danger in the use of paper money, however, always is the inclination, so easy to yield to, to issue far more paper than the value of the property behind it. This proved a temptation that the revolutionary assemblies did not have strength of mind or will to resist. At first the assignats were issued in limited quantities as the state needed the money, and the public willingly accepted them, But later larger and larger emissions were made, far out of proportion to the value of the national domains. This meant the rapid depreciation of the paper. People would not accept it at its face value, as they had at first been willing to do. The value of the church property was estimated in 1789 as 4,000,000,000 francs. Between 1789 and 1796 over 45,000,000,000 of assignats were issued. In 1789 an assignat of 100 francs was accepted for 100 francs in coin. But by 1791 it had sunk from par to 82, and by 1796 to less than a franc. This was neither an honest nor an effective solution of the perplexing financial problem. It was evasion, it was in its essence repudiation. The Constituent Assembly did nothing toward solving the problem that had occasioned its meeting. It left the national finances in a worse welter than it had found them in.

Another piece of legislation concerning the church, much more serious in its effects upon the cause of reform, was the Civil Constitution of the Clergy. By act of the Assembly the number of dioceses was reduced from 134 to 83, one for each department. The bishops and priests were henceforth to be elected by the same persons who elected the departmental officials. Once elected, the bishops were to announce the fact to the Pope, who was not to have the right to approve or disapprove but merely to confirm. He was then to recognize them. If he refused, the ordinary courts could be invoked. The clergy were to receive salaries from the state, were, in other words, to become state officials. The income of most of the bishops would be greatly reduced, that of the parish priests considerably increased.

This law was not acceptable to sincere Catholics as it altered by act of politicians an organization that had hitherto been controlled absolutely from within. Bishops and priests were to be elected like other officials — that is, Protestants, Jews, free-thinkers might participate in choosing the religious functionaries of the Catholic Church. Judges, who might be infidels, might yet play a decisive part. The Pope was practically ignored. His nominal headship was not questioned. His real power was largely destroyed. He would be informed of what was happening; his approval would not be necessary.

The Assembly voted that all clergymen must take an oath to support this Civil Constitution of the Clergy. Only four of the 134 bishops consented to do so. Perhaps a third of the parish priests consented. Those who consented were called the juring, those who refused, the non-juring or refractory clergy. In due time elections were held as provided by the law and those elected were called the constitutional clergy. France witnessed the spectacle of two bodies of priests, one non-juring, chosen in the old way, the other elected by the voters indirectly. The scandal was great and the danger appalling, for religious discord was introduced into every city and hamlet. Faith supported the one body, the state supported the other — and the state embarked upon a long, gloomy, and unsuccessful struggle to impose its will in a sphere where it did not belong.

Most fatal were the consequences. One was that it made the position of Louis XVI, a sincere Catholic, far more difficult and exposed him to the charge of being an enemy of the Revolution, if he hesitated in his support of measures which he could not and did not approve. Another was that it provoked in various sections, notably in Vendee, the most passionate civil war France had ever known. Multitudes of the lower clergy, who had favored and greatly helped the Revolution so far, now turned against it for conscience' sake. We cannot trace in detail this lamentable chapter of history. Suffice it to say that the Constituent Assembly made no greater or more pernicious mistake. The church had, as the issue proved, immense spiritual influence over the peasants, the vast bulk of the population. Henceforth there was a divided allegiance — allegiance to the state, allegiance to the church. Men had to make an agonizing choice. The small counter-revolutionary party of the nobles, hitherto a staff of officers without an army, was now reinforced by thousands and millions of recruits, prepared to face any sacrifices. And worldly intriguers could draw on this fund of piety for purposes that were anything but pious. The heat generated by politics is sufficient. There was no need of increasing the temperature by adding the heat of religious controversy. French Revolution or eternal damnation, such was the hard choice placed before the devout.

"I would rather be King of Metz than remain King of France in such a position," said Louis XVI, as he signed the decree requiring an oath to the Civil Constitution of the Clergy, "but this will end soon." The meaning of which remark was that the King was now through with his scruples, that he was resolved to call the monarchs of Europe to his aid, that he was determined to escape from this coil of untoward events that was binding him tighter and tighter, threatening soon to strangle him completely. The idea of a royal flight was not new. Marie Antoinette had thought of it long before. Mirabeau had counseled it under certain conditions which, however, were no longer possible. The nobles who had fled from France, some of them after the fall of the Bastille, more of them after the war upon the chateaux, hung upon the fringes of the kingdom, in Belgium, in Piedmont, and particularly in the petty German states that lined the fabled banks of the Rhine, eager to have the King come to them, eager to embroil Europe with France, that thus they might return to Paris with the armies that would surely be easily victorious, and set back the clock to where it stood in 1789, incidentally celebrating that happy occurrence by miscellaneous punishment of all the notable revolutionists, so that henceforth imaginative spirits would hesitate before again laying impious hands upon the Lord's anointed, upon kings by divine right, upon nobles reposing upon rights no less sacred, upon the holy clergy. The Count of Artois, the proud and empty-headed brother of the King, one of the first to emigrate, had said: "We shall return within three months." As a matter of fact he was to return only after twenty-three years, a considerable miscalculation, pardonable no doubt in that extraordinary age in which everyone miscalculated.

Louis XVI, wounded in his conscience, now planned to escape from Paris, to go to the eastern part of France, where there were French troops on which he thought he could rely. Then, surrounded by faithful adherents, he could reassume the kingly role and come back to Paris, master of the situation.

Disguised as a valet the King, accompanied by the Queen, disguised as a Russian lady, escaped from the Tuileries in the night of June 20, 1791, in a clumsy coach. All the next day they rolled over the white highways of Champagne under a terrible sun, reaching at about midnight the little village of Varennes, not far from the frontier. There they were recognized and arrested. The National Assembly sent three commissioners to bring them back. The return was for these two descendants of long lines of kings a veritable ascent of Calvary. Outrages, insults, jokes, ignominies of every kind were hurled at them by the crowds that thronged about them in the villages through which they passed — a journey without rest, uninterrupted, under the annihilating heat, the suffocating dust of June. Reaching Paris they were no longer overwhelmed with insults, but were received in glacial silence by enormous throngs who stood with hats on, as the royal coach passed by. The King was impassive, but "our poor Queen," so wrote a friend, "bowed her head almost to her knees." Rows of national guards stood, arms grounded, as at funerals. At seven o'clock that night they were in the Tuileries once more. Marie Antoinette had in these few days of horror grown twenty years older. Her hair had turned quite white, "like the hair of a woman of seventy."

The consequences of this woeful misadventure were extremely grave. Louis XVI had shown his real feelings. The fidelity of his people to him was not entirely destroyed but was irremediably shaken. They no longer believed in the sincerity of his utterances, his oaths to support the constitution. The Queen was visited with contumely, being regarded as the arch-conspirator. The throne was undermined. A republican party appeared. Before this no one had considered a republic possible in so large a country as France. Republics were for small states like those of ancient Greece or medieval Italy. Even the most violent revolutionists, Robespierre, Danton, Marat, were, up to this time, monarchists. Now, however, France had a little object-lesson. During the absence of the King, the government of the Assembly continued to work normally. In the period following, during which Louis XVI was suspended from the exercise of his powers, government went on without damage to the state. A king was evidently not indispensable. It has been correctly stated that the flight to Varennes created the republican party in France, a party that has had an eventful history since then, and has finally, after many vicissitudes, established its regime.

But this republican party was very small. The very idea of a republic frightened the Constituent Assembly, even after the revelation of the faithlessness of the King. Consequently, in a revulsion of feeling, the Assembly, after a little, restored Louis XVI to his position, finished the constitution, accepted his oath to support it, and on September 30, 1791, this memorable body declared its mission fulfilled and its career at an end.

The National Assembly before adjournment committed a final and unnecessary mistake. In a mood of fatal disinterestedness it voted that none of its members should be eligible to the next legislature or to the ministry. Thus the experience of the past two years was thrown away and the new constitution was intrusted to hands entirely different from those that had fashioned it.

# CHAPTER IV

## THE LEGISLATIVE ASSEMBLY

THE constitution was now to be put into force. France was to make the experiment of a constitutional monarchy in place of the old absolute monarchy, gone forever. In accordance with the provisions of the document a legislature was now chosen. Its first session was held October 1, 1791. Elected for a two-year term, it served for less than a single year. Expected to inaugurate an era of prosperity and happiness by applying the new principles of government in a time of peace, to consolidate the monarchy on its new basis, it was destined to a stormy life and to witness the fall of the monarchy in irreparable ruin. A few days before it met Paris, adept, as always, in the art of observing fittingly great national occasions, had celebrated "the end of the Revolution." The old regime was buried. The new one was now to be installed.

But the Revolution had not ended. Instead, it shortly entered upon a far more critical stage. The reasons for this unhappy turn were grave and numerous. They were inherent in the situation, both in France and in Europe. Would the King frankly accept his new position, with no mental reservations, with no secret determinations, honestly, entirely? If so, and if he would by his conduct convince his people of his loyalty to his word, of his intention to rule as a constitutional monarch, to abide by the reforms thus far accomplished, with no thought of upsetting the new system, then there was an excellent chance that the future would be one of peaceful development, for France was thoroughly monarchical in tradition, in feeling, and in conviction. The Legislative Assembly was as monarchical in its sentiments as the Constituent had been. But if the King's conduct should arouse the suspicion that he was intriguing to restore the Old Regime, that his oaths were insincere, then the people would turn against him and the experiment of a constitutional monarchy would be hazarded. France had no desire to be a republic, but it had also a fixed and resolute aversion to the Old Regime.

Inevitably, since the flight to Varennes, suspicion of Louis XVI was widespread. The suspicion was not dissipated by wise conduct on his part, but was increased in the following months to such a pitch that the revolutionary fever had no chance to subside but necessarily mounted steadily. The King's views were inevitably colored by his hereditary pretensions. Moreover, as we have seen, the religious question had been injected into the Revolution in so acute a form that his conscience as a Catholic was outraged. It was this that strained to the breaking point the relations of the Legislative Assembly and Louis XVI. The Civil Constitution of the Clergy gave rise to a bitter and distressing civil war. In the great province of Vendee several thousand peasants, led by the refractory or non-juring priests, rose against the elected, constitutional priests and drove them out of the pulpits and churches. When national guards were sent among them to enforce the law they flew to arms against them and civil war began.

The Assembly forthwith passed a decree against the refractory priests, which only made a bad matter worse. They were required to take the oath to the Civil Constitution within a week. If they refused they would be considered "suspicious" characters, their pensions would be suppressed, and they would be subject to the watchful and hostile surveillance of the government. Louis XVI vetoed this decree, legitimately using the power given him by the constitution. This veto, accompanied by others, offended public opinion, and weakened the King's hold upon France. It would have been better for Louis had he never been given the veto power, since every exercise of it placed him in opposition to the Assembly and inflamed party passions.

The other decrees which he vetoed concerned the royal princes and the nobles who had emigrated from France, either because they no longer felt safe there, or because they thought that by going to foreign countries they might induce their rulers to intervene in French affairs and restore the Old Regime. This was wanton playing with fire. For the effect on France might be the very opposite of that intended. It might so heighten and exasperate popular feeling that the monarchy would be in greater danger than if left alone. This emigration, mostly of the privileged classes, had begun on the morrow of the storming of the Bastille. The Count d'Artois, younger brother of Louis XVI, had left France on July 15, 1789. The emigration became important in 1790, after the decree abolishing all titles of nobility, a decree that deeply wounded the pride of the nobles, and it was accelerated in 1791, after the flight to Varennes and the suspension of the King. It was later augmented by great numbers of non-juring priests and of bourgeois, who put their fidelity to the Catholic Church above their patriotism.

It has been estimated that during the Revolution a hundred and fifty thousand people left France in this way. Many of them went to the little German states on the eastern frontier. There they formed an army of perhaps 20,000 men. The Count of Provence, elder brother of Louis XVI, was the titular leader and claimed that he was the regent of France on the ground that Louis XVI was virtually a prisoner. The emigres ceaselessly intrigued in the German and European courts, trying to instigate their rulers to invade France, particularly the rulers of Austria and Prussia, important military states, urging that the fate of one monarch was a matter that concerned all monarchs, for sentimental reasons and for practical, since, if the impious revolution triumphed in France, there would come the turn of the other kings for similar treatment at the hands of rebellious subjects. In 1791 the emigres succeeded in inducing the rulers of Austria and Prussia to issue the Declaration of Pillnitz announcing that the cause of Louis XVI was the cause of all the monarchs of Europe. This declaration was made conditional upon the cooperation of all the countries and, therefore, it was largely bluster and had no direct importance. It was not sufficient to bring on war. But it angered France and increased suspicion of the King. The Legislative Assembly passed two decrees, one declaring that the Count of Provence would be deprived of his eventual rights to the throne if he did not return to France within two months, the other declaring that the property of the emigres would be confiscated and that they themselves would be treated as enemies, as guilty of treasonable conspiracy, if their armaments were not dispersed by January 1, 1792; also stating that the French princes and public officials who had emigrated should be likewise regarded as conspiring against the state and would be exposed to the penalty of death, if they did not return by the same date. Louis XVI vetoed these decrees. He did, however, order his two brothers to return to France. They refused to obey out of "tenderness" for the King. The Count of Provence, who had a gift for misplaced irony and impertinence, saw fit to exercise it in his reply to the Assembly's summons. If this was not precisely pouring oil upon troubled waters, it was precisely adding fuel to a mounting conflagration, perhaps a natural mode of action for those who are dancing on volcanoes. Prudent people prefer to do their dancing elsewhere.

More serious were the war clouds that were rapidly gathering. At the beginning of the Revolution nothing seemed less likely than a conflict between France and Europe. France was pacifically inclined, and there were no outstanding subjects of dispute. Moreover the rulers of the other countries were not at all anxious to intervene. They were quite willing to have France occupied exclusively with domestic problems, as thus the field would be left open for their intrigues. They were meditating the final partition of Poland and wished to be left alone while they committed that crowning iniquity. But gradually they came to see the menace to themselves in the new principles proclaimed by the French, principles of the sovereignty of the people and of the equality of all citizens. Their own subjects, particularly the peasants and the middle classes, were alarmingly enthusiastic over the achievements of the French. If such principles should inspire the same deeds as in France, the absolute monarchy of Louis XVI would not be the only one to suffer a shock.

Just as the sovereigns were being somewhat aroused from this complacent indifference in regard to their neighbor's principles, a change was going on in France itself, where certain parties were beginning to proclaim their duty to share their happiness with other peoples, in other words, to conduct a propaganda for their ideas outside of France. They were talking of the necessity of warring against tyrants, and of liberating peoples still enslaved.

Thus on both sides the temper was becoming warlike. When such a mood prevails it is never difficult for willing minds to find sufficient pretexts for an appeal to arms. Moreover each side had a definite and positive grievance. France, as we have seen, viewed with displeasure and concern the formation of the royalist armies on her eastern borders, with the connivance, or at least the consent, of the German princes. On the other hand, the German Empire had a direct grievance against France. When Alsace became French in the seventeenth century, a number of German princes possessed lands there and were, in fact, feudal lords. They still remained princes of the German Empire and their territorial rights were guaranteed by the treaties. Only they were at the same time vassals of the King of France, doing homage to him and collecting feudal dues, as previously. When the French abolished feudal dues, as we have seen, August 4, 1789, they insisted that these decrees applied to Alsace as well as to the rest of France. The German princes protested and asserted that the decrees were in violation of the treaties of Westphalia. The German Diet espoused their cause. The Constituent Assembly insisted upon maintaining its laws, in large measure, but offered to modify them. The Diet refused, demanding the revocation of the obnoxious laws and the restoration of the feudal dues in Alsace. The controversy was full of danger for the reason that there were many people, both in France and in the other countries, who were anxious for war and who would use any means they could to bring it about. The gale was gathering that was to sweep over Europe in memorable devastation for nearly a quarter of a century.

The Legislative Assembly was composed of inexperienced men, because of the self-denying ordinance passed in the closing hours of the Constituent Assembly. Yet this Assembly was vested by the new constitution with powers vastly overshadowing those left with the King. Yet it was suspicious of the latter, as it had no control over the ministry and as it was the executive that directed the relations with foreign countries.

There were, moreover, certain new forces in domestic politics of which the world was to hear much in the coming months. Certain political clubs began to loom up threateningly as possible rivals even of the Assembly. The two most conspicuous were the Jacobin and the Cordelier clubs. These had originated at the very beginning of the Revolution, but it was under the Legislative Assembly and its successor that they showed their power.

The Jacobin Club was destined to the greater notoriety. It was composed of members of the Assembly and of outsiders, citizens of Paris. As a political club the members held constant sessions and debated with great zeal and freedom the questions that were before the Assembly. Its most influential leader at this time was Robespierre, a radical democrat but at the same time a convinced monarchist, a vigorous opponent of the small republican party which had appeared momentarily at the time of the epoch-making flight to Varennes. The Jacobin Club grew steadily more radical as the Revolution progressed and as its more conservative members dropped out or were eliminated. It also rapidly extended its influence over all France. Jacobin clubs were founded in over 2,000 cities and villages. Affiliated with the mother club in Paris, they formed a vast network, virtually receiving orders from Paris, developing great talent for concerted action. The discipline that held this voluntary organization together was remarkable and rendered it capable of great and decisive action. It became a sort of state within the state, and moreover, within a state which was as decentralized and ineffective as it was itself highly centralized and rapid and thorough in its action. The Jacobin Club gradually became a rival of the Assembly itself and at times exerted a preponderant influence upon it, yet the Assembly was the legally constituted government of all France.

The Cordelier Club was still more radical. Its membership was derived from a lower social scale. It was more democratic. Moreover, since the flight to Varennes it was the hotbed of republicanism. Its chief influence was with the working classes of Paris, men who were enthusiastic supporters of the Revolution, anxious to have it carried further, easily inflamed against anyone who was accused as an enemy, open or secret, of the Revolution. These men were crude and rude but tremendously energetic. They were the stuff of which mobs could be made, and they had in Danton, a lawyer, with a power of downright and epigrammatic speech, an able, astute, and ruthless leader. The Cordelier Club, unlike the Jacobin, was limited to Paris; it had no branches throughout the departments. Like the Jacobins the Cordeliers contracted the habit of bringing physical pressure to bear upon the government, of seeking to impose their will upon that of the representatives of the nation, the King and the Assembly.

Here, then, were redoubtable machines for influencing the public. They would support the Assembly as long as its conduct met their wishes, but they were self-confident and self-willed enough to oppose it and to try to dominate it on occasion. Both were enthusiastic believers in the Revolution; both were lynx-eyed and keen-scented for any hostility to the Revolution, willing to go to any lengths to uncover and to crush those who should try to undo the reforms thus far accomplished. Both were suspicious of the King.

They had inflammable material enough to work upon in the masses of the great capital of France. And these masses were, as the months went by, becoming steadily more excitable and exalted in temper. They worshiped liberty frantically and they expressed their worship in picturesque and sinister ways. They considered themselves, called themselves the true "patriots," and, like all fanatics, they were highly jealous and suspicious of their more moderate fellow-citizens. The new wine, which was decidedly heady, was fermenting dangerously in their brains. They displayed the revolutionary colors, the tricolor cockade, everywhere and on all occasions. They adopted and wore the bonnet rouge or red cap, which resembled the Phrygian cap of antiquity, the cap worn by the slaves after their emancipation. This was now, as it had been then, the symbol of liberty.

This is the period, too, when we hear of the planting of liberty poles or trees everywhere amid popular acclamation and with festivities calculated to intensify the new-born democratic devotion. Even in dress the new era had its radical innovations and symbolism. The sans-culottes now set the style. They were the men who abandoned the old-style short breeches, the culottes, and adopted the long trousers hitherto worn only by workingmen and therefore a badge of social inferiority.

Such, then, was the new quality in the atmosphere, such were the new players who were grouped around the margins of the scene. Their influence was felt all through its year of fevered history by the Legislative Assembly, the lawful government of France. These men were all aglow with the great news announced in the Declaration of the Rights of Man, that the people are sovereign here below and that no divinity doth hedge about a King — that was sheer clap-trap which had imposed on mankind quite long enough. Now that France was delivered from this sorry hallucination, now that the darkness was dispelled, let the new principles be fearlessly applied!

The reaction of all this upon the Legislative Assembly was pronounced. One of the first actions of that Assembly was to abolish the terms, "Sire" and "Your Majesty," used in addressing the King. Another evidence that the new doctrine of the sovereignty of the people was not merely a rosy, yet unsubstantial, figment of the imagination, but was a definite principle intended to be applied to daily politics, was the fact that when dissatisfied with the Assembly, the people crowded into its hall more frequently, expressing their disapproval, voicing in unambiguous manner their desires, and the Assembly, which believed in the doctrine too, did not dare resent its application, did not dare assert its inviolability, as the representative of France, of law and order.

The signs of the times, then, were certainly not propitious for those who would undo the work of the Revolution, who would restore the King and the nobles to the position they had once occupied and had now lost. The pack would be upon them if they tried. The struggle would be with a rude and vigorous democracy in which reverence for the old had died, which was reckless of traditions, and was ready to suffer, and more ready to inflict suffering, if attempts were made to thwart it. Anything that looked like treachery would mean a popular explosion. Yet this moment, so inopportune, was being used by the King and Queen in secret but suspected machinations with foreign rulers, with a view to securing their aid in the attempt to recover the ground lost by the monarchy; was being used by the emigrant nobles in Coblenz and Worms for counter-revolutionary intrigues and for war-like preparations. Their only safe policy was a candid and unmistakable recognition of the new regime, but this was precisely what they were intellectually and temperamentally incapable of appreciating. They were playing with fire. This was all the more risky as many of their enemies were equally willing to play with the same dangerous element.

There was in the Legislative Assembly a group of men called the Girondists, because many of their leaders, Vergniaud, Isnard, Buzot and others, came from that section of France known as Gironde, in the region of Bordeaux. The Girondists have enjoyed a poetic immortality ever since imaginative histories of the Revolution issued from the pensive pen of the poet Lamartine, who portrayed them as pure and high-minded patriots caught in the swirl of a wicked world. The description was inaccurate. They were not disinterested martyrs in the cause of good government. They were a group of politicians whose discretion was not as conspicuous as their ambition. They paid for that vaulting emotion the price which it frequently exacts. They knew how to make their tragic exit from life bravely and heroically. They did not know, what is more difficult, how to make their lives wise and profitable to the world. They were a group of eloquent young men, led by a romantic young woman. For the real head of this group that had its hour upon the stage and then was heard no more in the deafening clamor of the later Revolution, was Madame Roland, their bright particular star. Theirs was a bookish outlook upon the world. They fed upon Plutarch, and boundless was their admiration for the ancient Greeks and Romans. They were republicans because those glorious figures of the earlier time had been republicans; also because they imagined that, in a republic, they would themselves find a better chance to shine and to irradiate the world. Dazzled by these prototypes, they burned with the spirit of emulation. The reader must keep steadily in mind that the Girondists and the Jacobins were entirely distinct groups. They were, indeed, destined later to be deadly rivals and enemies.

Such were the personages who played their dissimilar parts in the hot drama of the times. The stage was set. The background was the whole fabric of the European state system, now shaking unawares. The action began with the declaration of war by France against Francis II, ruler of Austria, and nephew of Marie Antoinette, a declaration which opened a war which was to be European and world-wide, which was to last twenty-three long years, was to deform and twist the Revolution out of all resemblance to its early promise, was, as by-products, to give France a republic, a Reign of Terror, a Napoleonic epic, a Bourbon overthrow and restoration, and was to end only with the catastrophic incident of Waterloo.

That war was precipitated by the French, who sent an ultimatum to the Emperor concerning the emigres. Francis replied by demanding the restoration to the German princes in Alsace of their feudal rights and, in addition, the repression in France "of anything that might alarm other states." War was declared on April 20, 1792. It was desired by all the parties of the Legislative Assembly. Only seven members voted against it. The supporters of the King wanted it, believing that it would enable him to recover power once more by rendering him popular as the leader in a victorious campaign and by putting at his disposal a strong military force. Girondists and Jacobins wanted it for precisely the opposite reason, as likely to prove that Louis was secretly a traitor, in intimate relations with the enemies of France. This once established, the monarchy could be swept aside and a republic installed. Only Robespierre and a few others opposed it on the ground that war always plays into the hands of the rich and powerful, that the people, on the other hand, the poor, always pay for it and lose rather than gain, that war is never in the interest of a democracy. They were, however, voices crying in the wilderness. There was a widespread feeling that the war was an inevitable clash between democracy, represented by France under the new dispensation, and autocracy, represented by the House of Hapsburg, a conflict of two eras, the past and the future. The national exaltation was such that the people welcomed the opportunity to spread abroad, beyond the borders of France, the revolutionary ideas of liberty and equality which they had so recently acquired and which they so highly prized. The war had some of the characteristics of a religious war, the same mental exaltation, the same dogmatic belief in the universal applicability of its doctrines, the same sense of duty to preach them everywhere; by force, if necessary.

This war was a startling and momentous turning-point in the history of the Revolution. It had consequences, some of which were foreseen, most of which were not. It reacted profoundly upon the

French and before it was over it compromised their own domestic liberty and generated a military despotism of greater efficiency than could be matched in the century-old history of the House of Bourbon.

First and foremost among the effects of the war was this: it swept the illustrious French monarchy clean away and put the monarchs to death. The war began disastrously. Instead of easily conquering Belgium, which belonged to Francis II, as they had confidently expected to, the French suffered severe reverses. One reason was that their army had been badly disorganized by the wholesale resignation or emigration of its officers, all noblemen. Another was the highly treasonable act of Louis XVI and Marie Antoinette, who informed the Austrians of the French plan of campaign. This treason of their sovereigns was not known to the French, but it was suspected, and it was none the less efficacious. At the same time that French armies were being driven back, civil war, growing out of the religious dissensions, was threatening in France. The Assembly, facing these troubles, indignantly passed two decrees, one ordering the deportation to penal colonies of all refractory or non-juring priests, the other providing for an army of 20,000 men for the protection of Paris.

Louis XVI vetoed both measures. Then the storm broke. The Jacobins inspired and organized a great popular demonstration against the King, the object being to force him to sign the decrees. Out from the crowded working-men's quarters emerged, on June 20, 1792, several thousand men, wearing the bonnet rouge, armed with pikes, and carrying standards with the Rights of Man printed on them. They went to the hall of the Assembly and were permitted to march through it, submitting a petition in which the pointed statement was made that the will of 25,000,000 people could not be balked by the will of one man. After leaving the hall the crowd went to the Tuileries, forced open the gates, and penetrated to the King's own apartments. The King for three hours stood before them, in the recess of a window, protected by some of the deputies. The crowd shouted, "Sign the decrees!" "Down with the priests!" One of the ringleaders of the demonstration, a butcher called Legendre, gained a notoriety that has sufficed to preserve his name from oblivion to this day, by shouting at the King, "Sir, you are a traitor, you have always deceived us, you are deceiving us still. Beware, the cup is full." Louis XVI refused to make any promises. His will, for once, did not waver. But he received a bonnet rouge and donned it and drank a glass of wine presented him by one of the crowd. The crowd finally withdrew, having committed no violence, but having subjected the King of France to bitter humiliation.

Immediately a wave of indignation at this affront and scandal swept over France and it seemed likely that, after all, it might redound to the advantage of Louis, increasing his popularity by the sympathy it evoked. But shortly other events supervened and his position became more precarious than ever. Prussia joined Austria in the war and the Duke of Brunswick, commander of the coalition armies, as he crossed the frontiers of France, issued a manifesto which aroused the people to a fever pitch of wrath. This manifesto had really been written by an emigre and it was redolent of the concentrated rancor of his class. The manifesto ordered the French to restore Louis XVI to complete liberty of action. It went further and virtually commanded them to obey the orders of the monarchs of Austria and Prussia. It announced that any national guards who should resist the advance of the allies would be punished as rebels and it wound up with the terrific threat that if the least violence or outrage should be offered to their Majesties, the King, the Queen, and the royal family, if their preservation and their liberty should not be immediately provided for, they, the allied monarchs, would "exact an exemplary and ever-memorable vengeance," namely, the complete destruction of the city of Paris.

Such a threat could have but one reply from a self-respecting people. It nerved them to incredible exertions to resent and repay the insult. Patriotic anger swept everything before it.

The first to suffer was the person whom the manifesto had singled out for special care, Louis XVI, now suspected more than ever of being the accomplice of these invaders who were breathing fire and destruction upon the French for the insolence of managing their own affairs as they saw fit. On August 10, 1792, another, and this time more formidable, insurrection occurred in Paris. At nine in the morning the crowd attacked the Tuileries. At ten the King and the royal family left the palace and sought safety in the Assembly. There they were kept in a little room, just behind the president's chair and there they remained for more than thirty hours. While the Assembly was debating, a furious combat was raging between the troops stationed to guard the Tuileries and the mob. Louis XVI, hearing the first shots, sent word to the guards to cease fire, but the officer who carried the command did not deliver it as long as he thought there was a chance of victory. The Swiss Guards were the heroes and the victims of that dreadful day. They defended the palace until their ammunition gave out and then, receiving the order to retire, they fell back slowly, but were soon overwhelmed by their assailants and 800 of them were shot down. The vengeance of the mob was frenzied. They themselves had lost hundreds of men. No quarter was given. More than 5,000 people were killed that day. The Tuileries was sacked and gutted. A sallow-complexioned young artillery officer, out of service, named Napoleon Bonaparte, was a spectator of this scene, from which he learned a few lessons which were later of value to him.

The deeds of August 10 were the work of the Revolutionary Commune of Paris. The former municipal government had been illegally overthrown by the Jacobins, who had then organized a new government which they entirely controlled. The Jacobins, the masters of Paris, had carefully prepared the insurrection of August 10 for the definite purpose of overthrowing Louis XVI. The menaces of the Duke of Brunswick had merely been the pretext. Now began that systematic dominance of Paris in the affairs of France which was to be brief but terrible. At the end of the insurrection the Commune forced the Legislative Assembly to do its wishes. Under this imperious and entirely illegal dictation the Assembly voted that the King should be provisionally suspended. This necessitated the making of a new constitution, as the Constitution of 1791 was monarchical. The present Assembly was a merely legislative body, not competent to alter the fundamental law. Therefore the Legislative Assembly, although its term was only half expired, decided to call a Convention to take up the matter of the constitution. Under orders from the Paris Commune it issued a decree to that effect and it made a further important decision. For elections to the Convention it abolished the property suffrage, established by the Constitution of 1791, and proclaimed universal suffrage. France, thus, on August 10, 1792, became a democracy.

The executive of France was thus overthrown. During the interval before the meeting of the Convention a provisional executive council, with Danton at the head, wielded the executive power, influenced by the Commune. The Assembly had merely voted the suspension of Louis XVI. The Commune, in complete disregard of law and in defiance of the Assembly, imprisoned the King and Queen in the Temple, an old fortress in Paris. The Commune also arrested large numbers of suspected persons.

This Revolutionary Commune, or City Council of Paris, was henceforth one of the powerful factors in the government of France. It, and not the Legislative Assembly, was the real ruler of the country between the suspension of the King on August 10 and the meeting of the Convention, September 20. It continued to be a factor, sometimes predominant, even under the Convention. For nearly two years, from August, 1792, until the overthrow of Robespierre on July 27, 1794, the Commune was one of the principal forces in politics. It signalized its advent by suppressing the freedom of the press, one of the precious conquests of the reform movement, by defying the committees of the Assembly when it chose, and by carrying through the infamous September Massacres, which left a monstrous and indelible stain upon the Revolution. The Commune was the representative of the lower classes and of the Jacobins. Its leaders were all extremely radical, and some were desperate characters who would stop at nothing to gain their ends.

The September Massacres grew out of the feeling of panic which seized the population of Paris as it heard of the steady approach of the Prussians and Austrians under the Duke of Brunswick. Hundreds of persons, suspected or charged with being real accomplices of the invaders, were thrown into prison. Finally the news reached Paris that Verdun was besieged, the last fortress on the road to the capital. If that should fall, then the enemy would have but a few days' march to accomplish and Paris would be theirs. The Commune and the Assembly made heroic exertions to raise and forward troops to the exposed position. The Commune sounded the tocsin or general alarm from the bell towers, and unfurled a gigantic black flag from the City Hall bearing the inscription, "The Country is in Danger." The more violent members began to say that before the troops were sent to the front the traitors within the city ought to be put out of the way. "Shall we go to the front, leaving 3,000 prisoners behind us, who may escape and murder our wives and children?" they asked. The hideous spokesman and inciter of the foul and cowardly slaughter was Marat, one of the most bloodthirsty characters of the time. The result was that day after day from September 2 to September 6 the cold-blooded murder of non-juring priests, of persons suspected or accused of "aristocracy," went on, without trial, the innocent and the guilty, men and women. The butchery was systematically done by men hired and paid by certain members of the Commune. The Legislative Assembly was too terrified itself to attempt to stop the infamous business, nor could it have done so had it tried. Nearly 1,200 persons were thus savagely hacked to pieces by the colossal barbarism of those days.

One consequence of these massacres was to discredit the cause of the Revolution. Another was to precipitate a sanguinary struggle between the Girondists, who wished to punish the "Septembrists" and particularly their instigator, Marat, and the Jacobins, who either defended them or assumed an attitude of indifference, urging that France had more important work to do than to spend its time trying to avenge men who were after all "aristocrats." The struggles between these factions were to fill the early months of the Convention which met on September 20, 1792, the elections having taken place under the gloomy and terrifying impressions produced by the September Massacres. On the same day, September 20, the Prussians were stopped in their onward march at Valmy. They were to get no further. The immediate danger was over. The tension was relieved.

# CHAPTER V

## THE CONVENTION

THE third Revolutionary assembly was the National Convention, which was in existence for three years, from September 20, 1792, to October 26, 1795. Called to draft a new constitution, necessitated by the suspension of Louis XVI, its first act was the abolition of monarchy as an institution. Before its final adjournment three years later it had drafted two different constitutions, one of which was never put in force, it had established a republic, it had organized a provisional government with which to face the appalling problems that confronted the country, it had maintained the integrity and independence of the country, threatened by complete dissolution, and had decisively defeated a vast hostile coalition of European powers. In accomplishing this gigantic task it had, however, made a record for cruelty and tyranny that left the Republic in deep discredit and made the Revolution odious to multitudes of men.

On September 21, 1792, the Convention voted unanimously that "royalty is abolished in France." The following day it voted that all public documents should henceforth be dated from "the first year of the French Republic." Thus unostentatiously did the Republic make its appearance upon the scene "furtively interjecting itself between the factions," as Robespierre expressed it. There was no solemn proclamation of the Republic, merely the indirect statement. As Aulard observes, the Convention had the air of saying to the nation, "There is no possibility of doing otherwise." Later the Republic had its heroes, its victims, its martyrs, but it was created in the first instance simply because there was nothing else to do. France had no choice in the matter. It merely accepted an imperative situation. A committee was immediately appointed to draw up a new constitution. Its work, however, was long postponed, for the Convention was distracted by a frenzied quarrel that broke out immediately between two parties, the Girondists and Jacobins. The latter party was often called the Mountain, because of the raised seats its members occupied. It is not easy to define the differences between these factions, which were involved in what was fundamentally a struggle for power. Both were entirely devoted to the Republic. Between the two factions there was a large group of members, who swung now this way and now that, carrying victory or defeat as they shifted their votes. They were the center, the Plain or the Marsh, as they were called because of the location of their seats in the convention hall.

On one point, the part that the city of Paris should be permitted to play in the government, the difference of opinion was sharp. The Girondists represented the departments and insisted that Paris, which constituted only one of the departments of the eighty-three into which France was divided, should have only one eighty-third of influence. They would tolerate no dictatorship of the capital. On the other hand the Jacobins drew their strength from Paris. They considered Paris the brain and the heart of the country, a center of light to the more backward provinces; they believed that it was the proper and predestined leader of the nation, that it was in a better position than was the country at large to appreciate the significance of measures and events, that it was, as Danton said, "the chief sentinel of the nation." The Girondists were anxious to observe legal forms and processes; they disliked and distrusted the frequent appeals to brute force. The Jacobins, on the other hand, were not so scrupulous. They were rude, active, forceful, indifferent to law, if law stood in the way. They were realists and believed in the application of force wherever and whenever necessary. Indeed their great emphasis was always put upon the necessity of the state. That justified everything. In other words anything was legitimate that might contribute to the safety or greatness of the Republic, whether legal or not.

But the merely personal element was even more important in dividing and envenoming these groups. The Girondists hated the three leaders of the Jacobins, Robespierre, Marat, and Danton. Marat and Robespierre returned the hatred, which was thus easily fanned to fever heat. Danton, a man of coarse fiber but large mould, above the pettiness of jealousy and pique, thought chiefly and instinctively only of the cause, the interest of the country at the given moment. He had no scruples, but he had a keen sense for the practical and the useful. He was anxious to work with the Girondists, anxious to smooth over situations, to avoid extremes, to subordinate persons to measures, to ignore the spirit of faction and intrigue, to keep all republicans working together in the same harness for the welfare of France. His was the spirit of easy-going compromise. But he met in the Girondists a stern, unyielding opposition. They would have nothing to do with him, they would not co-operate with him, and they finally ranged him among their enemies, to their own irreparable harm and to his.

The contest between these two parties grew shriller and more vehement every day, ending in a life and death struggle. It began directly after the meeting of the Convention, in the discussion as to what should be done with Louis XVI, now that monarchy was abolished and the monarch a prisoner of state.

The King had unquestionably been disloyal to the Revolution. He had given encouragement to the emigres and had entered into the hostile plans of the enemies of France. After the meeting of the Convention a secret iron box, fashioned by his own hand, had been discovered in the Tuileries containing documents which proved beyond question his treason. Ought he to have the full punishment of a traitor or had he been already sufficiently punished, by the repeated indignities to which he had been subjected, by imprisonment, and by the loss of his throne? Might not the Convention stay its hand, refrain from exacting the full measure of satisfaction from one so sorely visited and for whom so many excuses lay in the general goodness of his character and in the extraordinary perplexities of his position, perplexities which might have baffled a far wiser person, at a time when the men of clearest vision saw events as through a glass, darkly? But mercy was not in the hearts of men, particularly of the Jacobins, who considered Louis the chief culprit and unworthy of consideration. The Jacobins at first would not hear even of a trial. Robespierre demanded that the King be executed forthwith by a mere vote of the Convention, and Saint-Just, a satellite of Robespierre, recalled that "Caesar was despatched in the very presence of the Senate without other formality than twenty-two dagger strokes." But Louis was given a trial, a trial, however, before a packed jury, which had already shown its hatred of him, before men who were at the same time his accusers and his judges. The trial lasted over a month, Louis himself appearing at the bar, answering the thirty-three questions that were put to him and which covered his conduct during the Revolution. His statements were considered unsatisfactory. Despite the eloquent defense of his lawyer the Convention voted on January 15, 1793, that "Louis Capet" was "guilty of conspiracy against the liberty of the nation and of a criminal attack upon the safety of the state." The vote was unanimous, a few abstaining from voting but not one voting in the negative. Many of the Girondists then urged that the sentence be submitted to the people for their final action. Robespierre combated this idea with vigor, evidently fearing that the people would not go the whole length. This proposition was voted down by 424 votes against 283.

What should be the punishment? Voting on this question began at eight o'clock in the evening of January 16, 1793. During twenty-four hours the 721 deputies present mounted the platform one after the other, and announced their votes to the Convention. At eight o'clock on the evening of the 17th the vote was completed. The president announced the result. Number voting 721; a majority 361. For death 387; against death, or for delay, 334.

On Sunday, January 2ist, the guillotine was raised in the square fronting the Tuileries. At ten o'clock Louis mounted the fatal steps with courage and composure. He was greater on the scaffold than he had been upon the throne. He endeavored to speak. "Gentlemen, I am innocent of that of which I am accused. May my blood assure the happiness of the French." His voice was drowned by a roll of drums. He died with all the serenity of a profoundly religious man.

The immediate consequence of the execution was a formidable increase in the number of enemies France must conquer if she were to live, and an intensification of the passions involved. France was at war with Austria and Prussia. Now England, Russia, Spain, Holland, and the states of Germany and Italy entered the war against her, justifying themselves by the "murder of the King," although all had motives much more practical than this sentimental one. It was an excellent opportunity to gain territory from a country which was plainly in process of dissolution. Civil war, too, was added to the turmoil, as the peasants of the Vendee, 100,000 strong, rose against the republic which was the murderer of the king and the persecutor of the church. Dumouriez, an able commander of one of the French armies, was plotting against the Convention and was shortly to go over to the enemy, a traitor to his country.

The ground was giving way everywhere. The Convention stiffened for the fray, resolved to do or die, or both, if necessary. No government was ever more energetic or more dauntless. It voted to raise 300,000 troops immediately. It created a committee of General Security, a committee of Public Safety, a Revolutionary Tribunal, all parts of a machine that was intended to concentrate the full force of the nation upon the problem of national salvation and the annihilation of the Republic's enemies, whether foreign or domestic.

But while it was doing all this the Convention was floundering in the bog of angry party politics. Discussion was beginning its work of dividing the republicans, preparatory to consuming them. The first struggle was between the Girondists and the Jacobins. The Girondists wished to punish the men who had been responsible for the September Massacres. They wished to punish the Commune for numerous illegal acts. They hated Marat and were able to get a vote from the Convention sending him before the Revolutionary Tribunal, expecting that this would be the end of him. Instead, he was acquitted and became the hero of the populace of Paris, more powerful than before and now wilder than ever in his denunciations. Sanguinary Marat, feline Robespierre, were resolved on the annihilation of the Girondists. Danton, thinking of France and loathing all this discord, when the nation was in danger, all this exaggeration of self, this contemptible carnival of intrigue, thinking that Frenchmen had enemies enough to fight without tearing each other to pieces, tried to play the peacemaker. But he had the fate that peacemakers frequently have. He accomplished nothing for France and made enemies for himself.

The Commune, which supported the Jacobins, and which idolized Marat and respected Robespierre, intervened in this struggle, using, to cut it short, its customary weapon, physical force. It organized an insurrection against the Girondists, a veritable army of 80,000 men with sixty cannon. Marat, himself a member of the Convention, climbed to the belfry of the City Hall and with his own hand sounded the tocsin. This was Marat's day. He, self-styled Friend of the People, was the leader of this movement from the beginning to the end of the fateful June 2, 1793. The Tuileries, where the Convention sat, was surrounded by the insurrectionary troops. The Convention was the prisoner of the Commune, the Government of France at the mercy of the Government of Paris. The Commune demanded the expulsion of the Girondist leaders from the Convention. The Convention protested indignantly against the conduct of the insurgents. Its members resolved to leave the hall in a body. They were received with mock deference by the insurgents. The demand of their president that the troops disperse was bluntly refused until the Girondists who had been denounced should be expelled. The Convention was obliged to return to its hall conquered and degraded and to vote the arrest of twenty-nine Girondists. For the first time in the Revolution the assembly elected by the voters of France was mutilated. Violence had laid its hand upon the sovereignty of the people in the interest of the rule of a faction. The victory of the Commune was the victory of the Jacobins, who, by this treason to the nation, were masters of the Convention.

But not yet masters of the country. Indeed this high-handed crime of June 2 aroused indignation and resistance throughout a large section of France. Had the departments no rights which the Commune of Paris was bound to respect? The Girondists called the departments to arms against this tyrannical crew. They responded with alacrity, exasperated and alarmed. Four of the largest cities of France, Lyons, Marseilles, Bordeaux, and Caen, took up arms, and civil war, born of politics, added to the civil war born of religion in the Vendee, and to the ubiquitous foreign war, made confusion worse confounded. In all some sixty departments out of eighty-three participated in this movement, three-fourths of France. To meet this danger, to allay this strong distrust of Paris felt by the departments, to show them that they need not fear the dictatorship of the Commune, the Convention drafted in great haste the constitution which it had been summoned to make, but which it had for months ignored in the heat of party politics. And the Constitution of 1793, the second in the history of the Revolution, guarded so carefully the rights of the departments and the rights of the people that it made Parisian dictation impossible.

The Constitution of 1793 established universal suffrage. It also carried decentralization farther than did the Constitution of 1791, which had carried it much too far. The Legislature was to be elected only for a year, and all laws were to be submitted to the people for ratification or rejection before being put into force. This is the first appearance of the referendum. The executive was to consist of twenty-four members chosen by the legislature out of a list drawn up by the electors and consisting of one person from each department.

This constitution worked like a charm in dissipating the distrust of the departments. Their rights could not be better safeguarded. Submitted to the voters the constitution was overwhelmingly ratified, over 1,000,000 votes in its favor, less than 12,000 in opposition. But this is the only way in which this constitution ever worked. So thoroughly did it decentralize the state, so weak did it leave the central government, that even those who had accepted it cordially saw that it could not be applied immediately, with foreign armies streaming into France from every direction. What was needed for the crisis as everyone saw, was a strong government. Consequently by general agreement the constitution was immediately suspended, as soon as it was made. The suspension was to be merely provisional. As soon as the crisis should pass it should be put into operation. Meanwhile this precious document was put into a box in the center of the convention hall and was much in the way.

To meet the crisis, to enable France to hew her way through the tangle of complexities and dangers that confronted her, a provisional government was created, a government as strong as the one provided by the constitution was weak, as efficient as that would have proved inefficient. The new system was frankly based on force, and it inaugurated a Reign of Terror which has remained a hissing and a byword among the nations ever since. This provisional or revolutionary government was lodged in the Convention. The Convention was the sole nerve center whence shot forth to the farthest confines of the land the iron resolutions that beat down all opposition and fired all energies to a single end. The Convention was dictator, and it organized a government that was more absolute, more tyrannical, more centralized than the Bourbon monarchy, in its palmiest days, had ever dreamed of being. Montesquieu's sacred doctrine of the separation of powers, which the Constituent Assembly had found so excellent, was ignored.

The machinery of this provisional government consisted of two important committees, appointed by the Convention, the Committee of Public Safety, and the Committee of General Security; also of representatives on mission, of the Revolutionary Tribunal, and of the political clubs and committees of surveillance in the cities and villages throughout the country.

The Committee of Public Safety consisted at first of nine, later of twelve members. Chosen by the Convention for a term of a month, they were, as a matter of fact, reflected month after month, changes only occurring when parties changed in the Assembly. Thus Danton, upon whose suggestion the original committee had been created, was not a member of the enlarged committee, reorganized after the expulsion of the Girondists. He was dropped because he censured the acts of June 2, and his enemy Robespierre became the leading member. At first this committee was charged simply with the management of foreign affairs and of the army, but in the end it became practically omnipotent, directing the state as no single despot had ever done, intervening in every department of the nation's affairs, even holding the Convention itself, of which in theory it was the creature, in stern and terrified subjection to itself. Installing itself in the palace of the Tuileries, in the former royal apartments, it developed a prodigious activity, framing endless decrees, tossing thousands of men to the guillotine, sending thousands upon thousands against the enemies of France, guiding, animating, tyrannizing ruthlessly a people which had taken such pains to declare itself free, only to find its fragile liberties, so resoundingly affirmed in the famous Declaration, ground to powder beneath this iron heel. No men ever worked harder in discharging an enormous mass of business of every kind than did the members of the Committee of Public Safety. Hour after hour, around a green table, they listened to reports, framed decrees, appointed officials. Sometimes overcome with weariness they threw themselves on mattresses spread upon the floor of their committee room, snatched two or three hours of sleep, then roused themselves to the racking work again. Under them was the Committee of General Security, whose business was really police duty, maintaining order throughout the country, throwing multitudes of suspected persons into prison, whence they emerged only to encounter another redoubtable organ of this government, the Revolutionary Tribunal.

This Tribunal had been created at Danton's suggestion. It was an extraordinary criminal court, instituted for the purpose of trying traitors and conspirators rapidly. No appeal could be taken from its decisions. Its sentences were always sentences of death. Later, when Robespierre dominated the Committee of Public Safety, the number of judges was increased and they were divided into four sections, all holding sessions at the same time. Appointed by the Committee, the Revolutionary Tribunal servilely carried out its orders. It acted with a rapidity that made a cruel farce of justice. A man might be informed at ten o'clock that he was to appear before the Revolutionary Tribunal at eleven. By two o'clock he was sentenced, by four he was executed.

The Committee of Public Safety had another organ — the representatives on mission. These were members of the Convention sent, two to each department, and two to each army, to see that the will of the Convention was carried out. Their powers were practically unlimited. They could not themselves pronounce the sentence of death, but a word from them was sufficient to send to the Revolutionary Tribunal anyone who incurred their suspicion or displeasure.

There were other parts of this governmental machinery, wheels within wheels, revolutionary clubs, affiliated with the Jacobin Club in Paris, revolutionary committees of surveillance. Through them the will of the great Committee of Public Safety penetrated to the tiniest hamlet, to the remotest corner of the land. The Republic was held tight in this closely-woven mesh.

This machinery was created to meet a national need, of the most pressing character. The country was in danger, in direst danger, of submersion under a flood of invasion; also in danger of disruption from within. The authors of this system were originally men who appreciated the critical situation, who grasped facts as they were, who were resolute to put down every foreign and domestic enemy, and who thrilled the people with their appeals to boundless, self-sacrificing patriotism. Had this machinery been used in the way and for the purpose intended, it is not likely that it would have enjoyed the dismal, repellent reputation with posterity which it has enjoyed. France would have willingly endured and sanctioned a direct and strong government, ruthlessly subordinating personal happiness and even personal security to the needs of national welfare. No cause could be higher, and none makes a wider or surer appeal to men. But the system was not restricted to this end. It was applied to satisfy personal and party intrigues and rancors, it was used to further the ambitions of individuals, it was crassly distorted and debased. The system did not spring full-blown from the mind of any man or any group. It grew piece by piece, now this item being added, now that. Those who fashioned it believed that only by appealing to or arousing one of the emotions of men, fear, could the government get their complete and energetic support. The success of the Revolution could not be assured simply by love or admiration of its principles and its deeds — that was proved by events, the difficulties had only increased. There were too many persons who hated the Revolution. But even these had an emotion that could be touched, the sense of fear, horror, dread. That, too, is a powerful incentive to action. "Let terror be the order of the day," such was the official philosophy of the creators of this government, and it has given their system its name. Punish disloyalty swiftly and pitilessly and you create loyalty, if not from love, at least from fear, which will prove a passable substitute.

The Committee of Public Safety and the Convention lost no time in striking a fast pace. To meet the needs of the war a general call for troops was issued. Seven hundred and fifty thousand men were secured. "What we need is audacity, and more audacity, and audacity always" was a phrase epitomizing this aspect of history, a phrase thrown out by Danton, a man who knew how to sound the bugle call, knew how to mint the passion of the hour in striking form and give it the impress of his dynamic personality. Carnot, one of the members of the Committee of Public Safety, performed herculean feats in getting this enormous mass of men equipped, disciplined, and officered. A dozen armies were the result and they were hurled in every direction at the enemies of France. Representatives of the Convention accompanied each general, demanding victory of him or letting him know that his head would fall if victory were not forthcoming. Some did fail, even under this terrific incentive, this literal choice between victory or death, and they went to the scaffold. It was an inhuman punishment but it had tremendous effects, inspiring desperate energy. The armies made superhuman efforts and were wonderfully successful. A group of fearless, reckless, and thoroughly competent commanders emerged rapidly from the ranks. We shall shortly observe the reaction of these triumphant campaigns upon the domestic political situation.

While this terrific effort to hurl back the invaders of France was going on, the Committee of Public Safety was engaged in a lynx-eyed, comprehensive campaign at home against all domestic enemies or persons accused of being such. By the famous law of "suspects," everyone in France was brought within its iron grip. This law was so loosely and vaguely worded, it indicated so many classes of individuals, that under its provisions practically any one in France could be arrested and sent before the Revolutionary Tribunal. All were guilty of treason, and punishable with death, who "having done nothing against liberty have nevertheless done nothing for it." No guilty, and also no innocent, man could be sure of escaping so elastic a law, or, if arrested, could expect justice from a court which ignored the usual forms of law, which, ultimately, deprived prisoners of the right to counsel, and which condemned them in batches. Yet the Declaration of the Rights of Man, which had seemed a new evangel to an optimistic world, had stated that henceforth no one should be arrested or imprisoned except in cases determined by law and according to the forms of law.

A tree is judged by its fruits. Consider the results in this case. In every city, town, and hamlet of France arrests of suspected persons were made en masse, and judgment and execution were rendered in almost the same summary and comprehensive fashion. Only a few instances can be selected from this calendar of crime. The city of Lyons had sprung to the defense of the Girondists after their expulsion from the Convention on June 2. It took four months and a half and a considerable army to put down the opposition of this, the second city of France. When this was accomplished the Convention passed a fierce resolution: "The city of Lyons is to be destroyed. Every house which was inhabited by the rich shall be demolished. There will remain only the homes of the poor, of patriots, and buildings especially employed for industries, and those edifices dedicated to humanity and to education." The name of this famous city was to be obliterated. It was henceforth to be known as the Liberated City (Commune affranchie). This savage sentence was not carried out, demolition on so large a scale not being easy. Only a few buildings were blown to pieces. But over 3,500 persons were arrested and nearly half of them were executed. The authorities began by shooting each one individually. The last were mowed down in batches by cannon or musketry fire. Similar scenes were enacted, though not on so extensive a scale, in Toulon and Marseilles. It was for the Vendee that the worst ferocities were reserved. The Vendee had been in rebellion against the Republic, and in the interest of counter-revolution. The people had been angered by the laws against the priests. Moreover the people of that section refused to fight in the Republic's armies. It was entirely legitimate for the government to crush this rebellion, and it did so after an indescribably cruel war, in which neither side gave quarter. Carrier, the representative on mission sent out by the Convention, established a gruesome record for barbarity. He did not adopt the method followed by the Revolutionary Tribunal in Paris, which at least pretended to try the accused before sentencing them to death. This was too slow a process. Prisoners were shot in squads, nearly 2,000 of them. Drowning was resorted to. Carrier's victims were bound, put on boats, and the boats then sunk in the river Loire. Women and children were among the number. Even the Committee of Public Safety was shocked at Carrier's fiendish ingenuity and demanded an explanation. He had the insolence to pretend that the drownings were accidental. "Is it my fault that the boats did not reach their destination?" he asked. The number of bodies in the river was so great that the water was poisoned and for that reason the city government of Nantes forbade the eating of fish. Carrier was later removed by the Committee, but was not further punished by it, though ultimately he found his way to the guillotine.

Meanwhile at Paris the Revolutionary Tribunal was daily sending its victims to the guillotine, after trials which were travesties of justice. Guillotines were erected in two of the public squares and each day saw its executions. Week after week went by, and head after head dropped into the insatiable basket. Many of the victims were emigres or non-juring priests who had come back to France, others were generals who had failed of the indispensable victory and had been denounced as traitors. Others still were persons who had favored the Revolution at an earlier stage and had worked for it, but who had later been on the losing side in the fierce party contests which had rent the Convention. Nowadays political struggles lead to the overthrow of ministers. But in France, as in Renaissance Italy, they led to the death of the defeated party, or at least of its leaders. As the blood-madness grew in intensity, it was voted by the Convention, in order to speed up the murderous pace, that the Revolutionary Tribunal after hearing a case for three days might then decide it without further examination if it considered "its conscience sufficiently enlightened."

The Girondists were conspicuous victims. Twenty-one of them were guillotined on October 31, 1793, among them Madame Roland, who went to the scaffold "fresh, calm, smiling," according to a friend who saw her go. She had regretted that she "had not been born a Spartan or a Roman," a superfluous regret, as was shown by the manner of her death, "at only thirty-nine," words with which she closed the passionate Memoirs she wrote while in prison. Mounting the scaffold she caught sight of a statue of liberty. "O Liberty, how they've played with you!" she exclaimed.

She had been preceded some days before by Marie Antoinette, the daughter of an empress, the wife of a king, child of fortune and of misfortune beyond compare. The Queen had been subjected to an obscene trial, accused of indescribable vileness, the corruption of her son. "If I have not answered," she cried, "it is because Nature herself rejects such a charge made against a mother: I appeal to all who are here." This woman's cry so moved the audience to sympathy that the officials cut the trial short, allowing the lawyers only fifteen minutes to finish. The Queen bore herself courageously. She did not flinch. She was brave to the end. Marie Antoinette has never ceased to command the sympathy of posterity, as her tragic story, and the fall to which her errors partly led and the proud and noble courage with which she met her mournful fate, have never ceased to move its pity and respect. She stands in history as one of its most melancholy figures.

Charlotte Corday, a Norman girl, who had stabbed the notorious Marat to death, thinking thus to free her country, paid the penalty with serenity and dignity. All through these months men witnessed a tragic procession up the scaffold's steps of those who were great by position or character or service or reputation; Bailly, celebrated as an astronomer and as the Mayor of Paris in the early Revolution; the Duke of Orleans, who had played a shameless part in the Revolution, having been demagogue enough to discard his name and call himself Philip Equality, and having infamously voted, as a member of the Convention, for the death of his cousin, Louis XVI; Barnave, next to Mirabeau one of the most brilliant leaders of the Constituent Assembly; and so it went, daily executions in Paris and yet others in the provinces. Some, fleeing the terror that walked by day and night, caught at bay, committed suicide, like Condorcet, last of the philosophers, and gifted theorist of the Republic. Still others wandered through the countryside haggard, gaunt, and were finally shot down, as beasts of the field. Yet all this did not constitute "the Great Terror," as it was called. That came later.

Thus far there was at least a semblance or pretense of punishing the enemies of the Republic, the enemies of France. But now these odious methods were to be used as a means of destroying political and personal enemies. Politics assumed the character and risks of war.

We have seen that since August 10, 1792, there were two powers in the state, the Commune or government of Paris and the Convention or government of France, now directed by the Committee of Public Safety. These two had in the main cooperated thus far, overthrowing the monarchy, overthrowing the Girondists. But now dissension raised its head and harmony was no more. The Commune was in the control of the most violent party that the Revolution had developed. Its leaders were Hebert and

Chaumette. Hebert conducted a journal, the Pere Duchesne, which was both obscene and profane and which was widely read in Paris by the lowest classes. Hebert and Chaumette reigned in the City Hall, drew their strength from the rabble of the streets which they knew how to incite and hurl at their enemies. They were ultra-radicals, audacious, truculent. They constantly demanded new and redoubled applications of terror. For a while they dominated the Convention. Carrier, one of the Convention's representatives on mission, was really a tool of the Commune.

It was the Commune which now forced the Convention to attempt the dechristianization of France. For this purpose a new calendar was desired, a calendar that should discard Sundays, saints' days, religious festivals, and set up novel and entirely secular divisions of time. Henceforth the month was to be divided, not into weeks, but into decades or periods of ten days. Every tenth day was to be the rest day. The days of the months were changed to indicate natural phenomena, July becoming Thermidor, or period of heat; April becoming Germinal, or budding time; November becoming Brumaire, or period of fogs. Henceforth men were to date, not from the birth of Christ, but from the birth of Liberty. The year One of Liberty began September 21, 1792. The world was young again. The day was divided into ten hours, not twenty-four, and the ten were subdivided and subdivided into smaller units. This calendar was made obligatory. But great was the havoc created by the new chronology. Parents were required to instruct their children in the new method of reckoning time. But the parents had been brought up on the old system and experienced much difficulty in telling what time of day it was according to the new terminology. Watchmakers were driven to add another circle to the faces of their watches. One circle carried the familiar set of figures, the other carried the new. Thus was one difficulty partially conjured away. The new calendar lasted twelve years. It was frankly and intentionally anti-Christian. The Christian era was repudiated.

More important was the attempt to improvise a new religion. Reason was henceforth to be worshiped, no longer the Christian God. A beginning was made in the campaign for dechristianization by removing the bells from the churches, "the Eternal's gewgaws," they were called, and by making cannon and coin out of them. Death was declared to be "but an eternal sleep" — thus Heaven, and Hell as well, was abolished. There was a demand that church spires be torn down "as by their domination over other buildings they seem to violate the principle of equality," and many were consequently sacrificed. This sorry business reached its climax in the formal establishment by the Commune of Paris of the Worship of Reason. On November 10, 1793, the Cathedral of Notre Dame was converted into a "Temple of Reason." The ceremony of that day has been famous for a century and its fame may last another. A dancer from the opera, wearing the three colors of the republic, sat, as the Goddess of Reason, upon the Altar of Liberty, where formerly the Holy Virgin had been enthroned, and received the homage of her devotees. After this many other churches in Paris, and even in the provinces, were changed into Temples of Reason. The sacred vessels used in Catholic services were burned or melted down. In some cases the stone saints that ornamented, or at least diversified, the facades of churches, were thrown down and broken or burned. At Notre Dame in Paris they were boarded over, and thus preserved for a period when their contamination would not be feared or felt. Every tenth day services were held. They might take the form of philosophical discourses or political, or the form of popular banquets or balls.

The proclamation of this Worship of Reason was the high-water mark in the fortunes of the Commune. The Convention had been compelled to yield, the Committee of Public Safety to acquiesce in conduct of which it did not approve. Robespierre was irritated, partly because he had a religion of his own which he preferred and which he wished in time to bring forward and impose upon France, partly because as a member of the great Committee he resented the existence of a rival so powerful as the Commune. The Hebertists had shot their bolt. Robespierre now shot his. In a carefully prepared speech he declared that "Atheism is aristocratic. The idea of a Supreme Being who watches over oppressed innocence and who punishes triumphant crime, is thoroughly democratic." He furtively urged on all attacks upon the blasphemous Commune as when Danton declared, "These anti-religious masquerades in the Convention must cease."

But Robespierre was the secret enemy of Danton as well, though for a very different reason. The Commune stood for the Terror in all its forms and demanded that it be maintained in all its vigor. On the other hand Danton, Camille Desmoulins, and their friends, ardent supporters of the Terror as long as it was necessary, believed that now the need for it had passed and wished its rigor mitigated and the system gradually abandoned. The armies of the Republic were everywhere successful, the invaders had been driven back, and domestic insurrections had been stamped out. Sick at heart of bloodshed now that it was no longer required, the Dantonists began to recommend clemency to the Convention. The Committee of Public Safety was opposed to both these factions, the Hebertists and the Dantonists, and Robespierre was at the center of an intrigue to ruin both. The description of the machinations and manoeuvers which went on in the Convention cannot be undertaken here. To make them clear would require much space. It must suffice to say that first the Committee directed all its powers against the Commune and dared on March 13, 1794, to order the arrest of Hebert and his friends. Eleven days later they were guillotined. The rivalry of the Commune was over. The Convention was supreme. But the Committee had no desire to bring the Terror to an end. Several of its members saw their own doom in any lessening of its severity. Looking out for their own heads, they therefore resolved to kill Danton, as the representative of the dangerous policy of moderation. This man who had personified as no one else had done the national temper in its crusade against the allied monarchs, who had been the very central pillar of the state in a terrible crisis, who, when France was for a moment discouraged, had nerved her to new effort by the electrifying cry, "We must dare and dare again and dare without end," now fell a victim to the wretched and frenzied internecine struggles of the politicians, because, now that the danger was over, he advocated, with his vastly heightened prestige, a return to moderation and conciliation. Terror as a means of annihilating his country's enemies he approved. Terror as a means of oppressing his fellow-countrymen, the crisis once passed, he deplored and tried to stop. He failed. The wheel was tearing around too rapidly. He was one of the tempestuous victims of the Terror. When he plead for peace, for a cessation of sanguinary and ferocious partisan politics, his rivals turned venomously, murderously against him. Conscious of his patriotism he did not believe that they would dare to strike him. A friend entered his study as he was sitting before the fire in revery and told him that the Committee of Public Safety had ordered his arrest. "Well, then, what then?" said Danton. "You must resist." "That means the shedding of blood, and I am sick of it. I would rather be guillotined than guillotine," he replied. He was urged to fly. "Whither fly?" he answered. "You do not carry your country on the sole of your shoe," and he muttered, "They will not dare, they will not dare."

But they did dare. The next day he was in prison. In prison he was heard to say, "A year ago I proposed the establishment of the Revolutionary Tribunal. I ask pardon for it, of God and man." And again, "I leave everything in frightful confusion; not one of them understands anything of government. Robespierre will follow me. I drag down Robespierre. One had better be a poor fisherman than meddle with the governing of men." On the scaffold he exclaimed, "Danton, no weakness!" His last words were addressed to the executioner. "Show my head to the people; it is worth showing."

The fall of Danton left Robespierre the most conspicuous person on the scene, the most influential member of the Convention and of the Committee of Public Safety. He was master of the Jacobins. The Commune was filled with his friends, anxious to do his bidding. The Revolutionary Tribunal was controlled and operated by his followers. For nearly four months, from April 5 to July 27, he was practically dictator.

A very singular despot for a people like the French. His qualities were not those which have characterized the leaders or the masses of that nation. The most authoritative French historian of this period, Aulard, notes this fact. As a politician Robespierre was "astute, mysterious, undecipherable." "What we see of his soul is most repellent to our French instincts of frankness and loyalty. Robespierre was a hypocrite and he erected hypocrisy into a system of government."

He had begun as a small provincial lawyer. He fed upon Rousseau, and was the narrow and anemic embodiment of Rousseau's ideas. He had made his reputation at the Jacobin Club, where he delivered speeches carefully retouched and finished, abounding in platitudes that pleased, entirely lacking in the fire, the dash, the stirring, impromptu phrases of a Mirabeau or a Danton. His style was correct, mediocre, thin, formal, academic. "Virtue" was his stock in trade and he made virtue odious by his everlasting talk of it, by his smug assumption of moral superiority, approaching even the hazardous pretension to perfection. He was forever singing his own praises with a lamentable lack of humor and of taste. "I have never bowed beneath the yoke of baseness and corruption," he said. He won the title of "The Incorruptible."

As a politician his policy had been to use up his enemies, and every rival was an enemy, by suggesting vaguely but opportunely that they were impure, corrupt, immoral, and by setting the springs in motion that landed them on the scaffold. He had himself stepped softly, warily, past the ambushes that lay in wait for the careless or the impetuous. By such processes he had survived and was now the man of the hour, immensely popular with the masses, and feared by those who disliked him. How would he use his power, his opportunity?

He used it, not to bring peace to a sadly distracted country, not to heal the wounds, not to clinch the work of the Revolution, but to attempt to force a great nation to enact into legislation the ideas of a highly sentimental philosopher, Rousseau. It was to be a Reign of Virtue. Robespierre's ambition was to make virtue triumphant, a laudable purpose, if the definition of virtue be satisfactory and the methods for bringing about her reign honorable and humane. But in this case they were not.

Robespierre stands revealed, as he also stands condemned, by the two acts associated with his career as dictator, the proclamation of a new religion and the Law of Prairial altering for the worst the already monstrous Revolutionary Tribunal. Robespierre had once said in public, "If God did not exist we should have to invent him." Fortunately for a man of such poverty of thought as he, he did not have to resort to invention but found God already invented by his idolized Rousseau. He devoted his attention to getting the Convention to give official sanction to Rousseau's ideas concerning the Deity. The Convention at his instigation formally recognized "the existence of the Supreme Being and the Immortality of the Soul." On June 8, a festival was held in honor of the new religion, quite as famous, in its way, as the ceremonies connected with the inauguration, a few months before, of the Worship of Reason. It was a wondrous spectacle, staged by the master hand of the artist David. A vast amphitheatre was erected in the gardens of the Tuileries. Thither marched the members of the Convention in solemn procession, carrying flowers and sheaves of grain, Robespierre at the head, for he was president that day and played the pontiff, a part which suited him. He set fire to colossal figures, symbolizing Atheism and Vice, and then floated forth upon a long rhapsody. "Here," he cried from the platform, "is the Universe assembled. O Nature, how sublime, how exquisite, thy power! How tyrants will pale at the tidings of our feast!" A hundred thousand voices chanted a sacred hymn which had been composed for the occasion and for which they had been training for a week. Robespierre stood the cynosure of all eyes, at the very summit of ambition, receiving boundless admiration as he thus inaugurated the new worship of the Supreme Being, and breathed the intoxicating incense that arose. Profound was the irony of this scene, the incredible culmination of a century of skepticism. Some ungodly persons made merry over this mummery, indulging in indiscreet gibes at "The Incorruptible's" expense. The power of sarcasm was not yet dead in France, as this man who never smiled now learned.

Two days later Robespierre caused a bill to be introduced into the Convention which showed that this delicate hand could brandish daggers as well as carry flowers and shocks of corn. The irreverent, the dangerous, must be swept like chaff into the burning pit. This bill, which became the Law of 22nd Prairial, made the procedure of the Revolutionary Tribunal more murderous still. The accused were deprived of counsel. Witnesses need not be heard in cases where the prosecutor could adduce any material or "moral" proof. Any kind of opposition to the government was made punishable with death. The question of guilt was left to the "enlightened conscience" of the jury. The jury was purged of all members who were supposed to be lukewarm toward Robespierre. The accused might be sent before this packed and servile court either by the Convention, or by the Committee of Public Safety, or by the Committee of General Security, or by the public prosecutor alone. In other words, any life in France was at the mercy of this latter official, Fouquier-Tinville, a tool of Robespierre. The members of the Convention itself were no safer than others, nor were the members of the great Committee, if they incurred the displeasure of the dictator.

Now began what is called the Great Terror, as if to distinguish it from what had preceded. In the thirteen months which had preceded the 22nd of Prairial 1,200 persons had been guillotined in Paris. In the forty-nine days between that date and the fall of Robespierre, on the 9th of Thermidor, 1,376 were guillotined. On two days alone, namely the 7th and 8th of July, 150 persons were executed. Day after day the butchery went on.

It brought about the fall of Robespierre. This hideous measure united his enemies, those who feared him because they stood for clemency, and those who feared him because, though terrorists themselves, they knew that he had marked them for destruction. They could lose no more by opposing him than by acquiescing, and if they could overthrow him they would gain the safety of their heads. Thus in desperation and in terror was woven a conspiracy not to end the Terror, but to end Robespierre.

The storm broke on July 27, 1794 (the 9th of Thermidor). When Robespierre attempted to speak in the Convention, which had cowered under him and at his demand had indelibly debased itself by passing the infamous law of Prairial, he was shouted down. Cries of "Down with the tyrant!" were heard. Attempting to arouse the people in the galleries, he this time met with no response. The magic was gone. There was a confused, noisy struggle, lasting several hours. Robespierre's voice failed him. "Danton's blood is choking him!" exclaimed one of the conspirators. Finally the Convention voted his arrest and that of his satellites, his brother, Saint-Just, and Couthon.

All was not yet lost. The Revolutionary Tribunal was devoted to Robespierre and, if tried, there was an excellent chance that he would be acquitted. The Commune likewise was favorable to him. It took the initiative. It announced an insurrection. Its agents broke into his prison, released him, and bore him to the City Hall. Thereupon the Convention, hearing of this act of rebellion, declared him and his associates outlaws. No trial therefore was necessary. As soon as re-arrested he would be guillotined. During the evening and early hours of the night a confused attempt to organize an attack against the Convention went on. But a little before midnight a drenching storm dispersed his thousands of supporters in the square. Moreover Robespierre hesitated, lacked the spirit of decision and daring. The whole matter was ended by the Convention sending troops against the Commune. At two in the morning these troops seized the Hotel de Ville and arrested Robespierre and the leading members of the Commune. Robespierre had been wounded in the fray, his jaw fractured by a bullet.

He was borne to the Assembly, which declined to receive him. "The Convention unanimously refused to let him be brought into the sanctuary of the law which he had so long polluted," so ran the official report of this session. That day he and twenty others were sent to the guillotine. An enormous throng witnessed the scene and broke into wild acclaim. On the two following days eighty-three more executions took place.

France breathed more freely. The worst, evidently, was over. In the succeeding months the system of the terror was gradually abandoned. This is what is called the Thermidorian reaction. The various branches of the terrible machine of government were either destroyed or greatly altered. A milder regime began. The storm did not subside at once, but it subsided steadily, though not without several violent shocks, several attempts on the part of the dwindling Jacobins to recover their former position by again letting loose the street mobs. The policy of the Convention came to be summed up in the cry "Death to the Terror and to Monarchy!" The Convention was now controlled by the moderates, but it was unanimously republican. Signs that a monarchical party was reappearing, demanding the restitution of the Bourbons, but not of the Old Regime, prompted the Convention to counter-measures designed to strengthen and perpetuate the Republic.

To accomplish this and thus prevent the relapse into monarchy, the Convention drew up a new constitution, the third in six years. Though the radicals of Paris demanded vociferously that the suspended Constitution of 1793 be now put into force, the Convention refused, finding it too "anarchical" a document. Instead, it framed the Constitution of 1795 or of the Year Three. Universal suffrage was abandoned, the motive being to reduce the political importance of the Parisian populace. Democracy, established on August 10, 1792, was replaced by a suffrage based upon property. There was practically no protest. The example of the American states was quoted, none of which at that time admitted universal suffrage. The suffrage became practically what it had been under the monarchical Constitution of 1791. The national legislature was henceforth to consist of two chambers, not one, as had its predecessors. The example of America was again cited. "Nearly all the constitutions of these states," said one member, "our seniors in the cause of liberty, have divided the legislature into two chambers; and the result had been public tranquillity." It was, however, chiefly the experience which France had herself had with single-chambered legislatures during the last few years that caused her to abandon that form. One of the chambers was to be called the Council of Elders. This was to consist of 250 members, who must be at least forty years of age, and be either married or widowers. The other, the Council of the Five Hundred, was to consist of members of at least thirty years of age. This council alone was to have the right to propose laws, which could, however, not be put into force unless accepted by the Council of Elders.

The executive power was to be exercised by a Directory, consisting of five persons, of at least forty years of age, elected by the Councils, one retiring each year. The example of America was again recommended, but was not followed because the Convention feared that a single executive, a president, might remind the French too sharply of monarchy or might become a new Robespierre.

The Constitution of 1795 was eminently the result of experience, not of abstract theorizing. It established a bourgeois republic, as the Constitution of 1791 had established a bourgeois monarchy. The Republic was in the hands, therefore, of a privileged class, property being the privilege.

But the Convention either did not wish or did not dare to trust the voters to elect whom they might desire to the new Councils. Was there not danger that they might elect monarchists and so hand over the new republican constitution to its enemies? Would the members of the Convention, who enjoyed power, who did not wish to step down and out, and yet who knew that they were unpopular because of the record of the Convention, stand any chance of election to the new legislature? Yet the habit of power was agreeable to them. Would the Republic be safe? Was it not their first duty to provide that it should not fall into hostile hands?

Under the influence of such considerations the Convention passed two decrees, supplementary to the constitution, providing that two-thirds of each Council should be chosen from the present members of the Convention.

The constitution was overwhelmingly approved by the voters, to whom it was submitted for ratification. But the two decrees aroused decided opposition. They were represented as a barefaced device whereby men who knew themselves unpopular could keep themselves in power for a while longer. Although the decrees were finally ratified, it was by much smaller majorities than had ratified the constitution. The vote of Paris was overwhelmingly against them.

Nor did Paris remain contented with casting a hostile vote. It proposed to prevent this consummation. An insurrection was organized against the Convention, this time by the bourgeois and wealthier people, in reality a royalist project. The Convention intrusted its defense to Barras as commander-in-chief. Barras, who was more a politician than a general, called to his aid a little Corsican officer twenty-five years old who, two years before, had helped recover Toulon for the Republic. This little Buona-Parte, for this is the form in which the famous name appears in the official reports of the day, was an artillery officer, a believer in the efficacy of that weapon. Hearing that there were forty cannon in a camp outside the city in danger of being seized by the insurgents, Bonaparte sent a young dare-devil cavalryman, Joachim Murat, to get them. Murat and his men dashed at full speed through the city, drove back the insurgents, seized the cannon and dragged them, always at full speed, to the Tuileries, which they reached by six o'clock in the morning. As one writer has said, "Neither the little general nor the superb cavalier dreamed that, in giving Barras cannon to be used against royalists, each was winning a crown for himself."

The cannon were placed about the Tuileries, where sat the Convention, rendering it impregnable. Every member of the Convention was given a rifle and cartridges. On the 13th of Vendemiaire (October 5) on came the insurgents in two columns, down the streets on both sides of the Seine. Suddenly at four-thirty in the afternoon a violent cannonading was heard. It was Bonaparte making his debut. The Convention was saved and an astounding career was begun. This is what Carlyle, in his vivid way, calls "the whiff of grapeshot which ends what we specifically call the French Revolution," an imaginative and inaccurate statement, quite characteristic of this vehement historian. Though it did not end the Revolution, it did, however, end one phase of it and inaugurated another.

Three weeks later, on October 26, 1795, the Convention declared itself dissolved. It had had an extraordinary history, only a few aspects of which have been described in this brief account. In the three years of its existence it had displayed prodigious activity along many lines. Meeting in the midst of appalling national difficulties born of internal dissension and foreign war, attacked by sixty departments of France and by an astounding array of foreign powers, England, Prussia, Austria, Piedmont, Holland, Spain, it had triumphed all along the line. Civil war had been stamped out and in the summer of 1795 three hostile states, Prussia, Holland, and Spain, made peace with France and withdrew from the war. France was actually in possession of the Austrian Netherlands and of the German provinces on the west bank of the Rhine. She had practically attained the so-called natural boundaries. War still continued with Austria and England. That problem was passed on to the Directory.

During these three years the Convention had proclaimed the Republic in the classic land of monarchy, had voted two constitutions, had sanctioned two forms of worship and had finally separated church and state, a thing of extreme difficulty in any European country. It had put a king to death, had organized and endured a reign of tyranny, which long discredited the very idea of a republic among multitudes of the French, and which immeasurably weakened the Republic by cutting off so many men who, had they lived, would have been its natural and experienced defenders for a full generation longer, since most of them were young. The Republic used up its material recklessly, so that when the man arrived who wished to end it and establish his personal rule, this sallow Italian Buona-Parte, his task was comparatively easy, the opposition being leaderless or poorly led. On the other hand, the Republic had had its thrilling victories, its heroes, and its martyrs, whose careers and teachings were to be factors in the history of France for fully a century to come.

The Convention had also worked mightily and achieved much in the avenues of peaceful development. It had given France a system of weights and measures, more perfect than the world had ever seen, the metric system, since widely adopted by other countries. It had laid the foundations and done the preliminary work for a codification of the laws, an achievement which Napoleon was to carry to completion and of which he was to monopolize the renown. It devoted fruitful attention to the problem of national education, believing, with Danton, that "next to bread, education is the first need of the people," and that there ought to be a national system, free, compulsory, and entirely secular. "The time has come," said the eloquent tribune, to establish the great principle which appears to be ignored, "that children belong to the Republic before they belong to their parents." A great system of primary and secondary education was elaborated, but it was not put into actual operation, owing to the lack of funds. On the other hand, much was done for certain special schools. Among the invaluable creations of the Convention were certain institutions whose fame has steadily increased, whose influence has been profound, the Normal School, the Polytechnic School, the Law and Medical Schools of Paris, the Conservatory of Arts and Crafts, the National Archives, the Museum of the Louvre, the National Library, and the Institute. While some of these had their roots in earlier institutions, all such were so reorganized and amplified and enriched as to make them practically new. To keep the balance of our judgment clear we should recall these imperishable services to civilization rendered by the same assembly which is more notorious because of its connection with the iniquitous Reign of Terror. The Republic had its glorious trophies, its honorable records, from which later times were to derive inspiration and instruction.

# CHAPTER VI

## THE DIRECTORY

THE Directory lasted from October 27, 1795, to November 19, 1799. It took its name from the form of the executive branch of the Republic, as determined by the Constitution of 1795. Its history of four years was troubled, uncertain, and ended in its violent overthrow.

Its first and most pressing problem was the continued prosecution of the war. As already stated, Prussia, Spain, and Holland had withdrawn from the coalition and made peace with the Convention. But England, Austria, Piedmont, and the lesser German states were still in arms against the Republic. The first duty of the Directory was, therefore, to continue the war with them and to defeat them. France had already overrun the Austrian Netherlands, that is, modern Belgium, and had declared them annexed to France. But to compel Austria, the owner, to recognize this annexation she must be beaten. The Directory therefore proceeded with vigor to concentrate its attention upon this object. As France had thrown back her invaders, the fighting was no longer on French soil. She now became the invader, and that long series of conquests of various European countries by aggressive French armies began, which was to end only twenty years later with the fall of the greatest commander of modern times, if not of all history. The campaign against Austria, planned by the Directory, included two parallel and aggressive movements against that country — an attack through southern Germany, down the valley of the Danube, ending, it was hoped, at Vienna. This was the campaign north of the Alps. South of the Alps, in northern Italy, France had enemies in Piedmont and again in Austria, which had possession of the central and rich part of the Po valley, namely, Lombardy, with Milan as the capital.

The campaign in Germany was confided to Jourdan and Moreau; that in Italy to General Bonaparte, who made of it a stepping-stone to fame and power incomparable.

Napoleon Bonaparte was born at Ajaccio in Corsica in 1769, a short time after the island had been sold by Genoa to France. The family was of Italian origin but had been for two centuries and a half resident in the island. His father, Charles Bonaparte, was of the nobility but was poor, indolent, pleasure-loving, a lawyer by profession. His mother, Laetitia Ramolino, was a woman of great beauty, of remarkable will, of extraordinary energy. Poorly educated, this "mother of kings" was never able to speak the French language without ridiculous mistakes. She had thirteen children, eight of whom lived to grow up, five boys and three girls. The father died when the youngest, Jerome, was only three months old. Napoleon, the second son, was educated in French military schools at Brienne and Paris, as a sort of charity scholar. He was very unhappy, surrounded as he was by boys who looked down upon him because he was poor while they were rich, because his father was unimportant while theirs belonged to the noblest families in France, because he spoke French like the foreigner he was, Italian being his native tongue. In fact he was tormented in all the ways of which schoolboys are past masters. He became sullen, taciturn, lived apart by himself, was unpopular with his fellows, whom, in turn, he despised, conscious, as he was, of powers quite equal to any of theirs, of a spirit quite as high. His boyish letters home were remarkably serious, lucid, intelligent. He was excellent in mathematics, and was fond of history and geography. At the age of sixteen he left the military school and became a second lieutenant of artillery. One of his teachers described him at this time as follows: "Reserved and studious, he prefers study to amusement of any kind and enjoys reading the best authors; is diligent in the study of the abstract sciences, caring little for anything else. He is taciturn and loves solitude, is capricious, haughty, and excessively self-centered. He talks little but is quick and energetic in his replies, prompt and incisive in repartee. He has great self-esteem, is ambitious, with aspirations that will stop at nothing. Is worthy of patronage."

Young Bonaparte read the intoxicating literature of revolt of the eighteenth century, Voltaire, Turgot, particularly Rousseau. "Even when I had nothing to do," he said later, "I vaguely thought that I had no time to lose." As a young sub-lieutenant he had a wretchedly small salary. "I have no resources here but work," he wrote his mother. "I sleep very little. I go to bed at ten, I rise at four. I have only one meal a day, at three o'clock." He read history extensively regarding it as "the torch of truth, the destroyer of prejudice." He tried his hand at writing, essays, novels, but particularly a history of Corsica, for at this time his great ambition was to be the historian of his native land. He hated France and dreamed of a war of independence for Corsica. He spent much time in Corsica, securing long furloughs, which, moreover, he overstayed. As a consequence he finally lost his position in the army, which, though poorly salaried, still gave him a living. He returned to Paris in 1792 hoping to regain it, but the disturbed state of affairs was not propitious. Without a profession, without resources, he was almost penniless. He ate in cheap restaurants. He pawned his watch — and, as an idle but interested spectator, he witnessed some of the famous "days" of the Revolution, the invasion of the Tuileries by the mob on the 20th of June, when Louis XVI was forced to wear the bonnet rouge, the attack of August 10th when he was deposed, the September Massacres. Bonaparte's opinion was that the soldiers should have shot a few hundred, then the crowd would have run. He was restored to his command in August, 1792. In 1793 he distinguished himself by helping recover Toulon for the Republic and in 1795 by defending the Convention against the insurrection of Vendemiaire, which was a lucky crisis for him.

Having conquered a Parisian mob, he was himself conquered by a woman. He fell madly in love with Josephine Beauharnais, a widow six years older than himself, whose husband had been guillotined a few days before the fall of Robespierre, leaving her poor and with two children. Josephine did not lose her heart, but she was impressed, indeed half terrified, by the vehemence of Napoleon's passion, the intensity of his glance, and she yielded to his rapid, impetuous courtship, with a troubled but vivid sense that the future had great things in store for him. "Do they" (the Directors) "think that I need their protection in order to rise?" he had exclaimed to her. "They will be glad enough someday if I grant them mine. My sword is at my side and with it I can go far." "This preposterous assurance," wrote Josephine, "affects me to such a degree that I can believe everything may be possible to this man, and, with his imagination, who can tell what he may be tempted to undertake?"

Two days before they were married Bonaparte was appointed to the command of the Army of Italy. His sword was at his side. He now unsheathed it and made some memorable passes. Two days after the marriage he left his bride in Paris and started for the front, in a mingled mood of desperation at the separation and of exultation that now his opportunity had come. Sending back passionate love-letters from every station, his spirit and his senses all on fire, feeling that he was on the very verge of achievement, he hastened on to meet the enemy and, as was quickly evident, "to tear the very heart out of glory." The wildness of Corsica, his native land, was in his blood, the land of fighters, the land of the vendetta, of concentrated passion, of lawless energy, of bravery beyond compare, concerning which Rousseau had written in happy prescience twenty years before, "I have a presentiment that this little island will someday astonish Europe." That day had come. The young eagle it had nourished was now preening for his flight, prepared to astonish the universe.

The difficulties that confronted Bonaparte were numerous and notable. One was his youth and another was that he was unknown. The Army of Italy had been in the field three years. Its generals did not know their new commander. Some of them were older than he and had already made names for themselves. They resented this appointment of a junior, a man whose chief exploit had been a street fight in Paris. Nevertheless when this slender, round-shouldered, small, and sickly-looking young man appeared they saw instantly that they had a master. He was imperious, laconic, reserved with them. "It was necessary," he said afterward, "in order to command men so much older than myself." He was only five feet two inches tall, but, said Massena, "when he put on his general's hat he seemed to have grown two feet. He questioned us on the position of our divisions, on the spirit and effective force of each corps, prescribed the course we were to follow, announced that he would hold an inspection on the morrow, and on the day following attack the enemy." Augereau, a vulgar and famous old soldier, full of strange oaths and proud of his tall figure, was abusive, derisive, mutinous. He was admitted to the General's presence and passed an uneasy moment. "He frightened me," said Augereau, "his first glance crushed me. I cannot understand it."

It did not take these officers long to see that the young general meant business and that he knew very thoroughly the art of war. His speech was rapid, brief, incisive. He gave his orders succinctly and clearly and he let it be known that obedience was the order of the day. The cold reception quickly became enthusiastic cooperation.

Bonaparte won ascendency over the soldiers with the same lightning rapidity. They had been long inactive, idling through meaningless manoeuvers. He announced immediate action. The response was instantaneous. He inspired confidence and he inspired enthusiasm. He took an army that was discouraged, that was in rags, even the officers being almost without shoes, an army on half-rations. He issued a bulletin which imparted to them his own exaltation, his belief that the limits of the possible could easily be transcended, that it is all a matter of will. He got into their blood and they tingled with impatience and with hope. "There was so much of the future in him," is the way Marmont described the impression. "Soldiers," so ran this bulletin, "soldiers, you are ill-fed and almost naked; the government owes you much, it can give you nothing. Your patience, the courage which you exhibit in the midst of these crags, are worthy of all admiration; but they bring you no atom of glory; not a ray is reflected upon you. I will conduct you into the most fertile plains in the world. Rich provinces, great cities will be in your power; there you will find honor, glory, and wealth. Soldiers of Italy, can it be that you will be lacking in courage or perseverance?"

Ardent images of a very mundane and material kind rose up before him and he saw to it that his soldiers shared them. By portraying very earthly visions of felicity Mahomet, centuries before, had stirred the Oriental zeal of his followers to marvelous effort and achievement. Bonaparte took suggestions from Mahomet on more than one occasion in his life.

Bonaparte's first Italian campaign has remained in the eyes of military men ever since a masterpiece, a classic example of the art of war. It lasted a year, from April, 1796, to April, 1797. It may be summarized in the words, "He came, he saw, he conquered." He confronted an allied Sardinian and Austrian army, and his forces were much inferior in number. His policy was therefore to see that his enemies did not unite, and then to beat each in turn. His enemies combined had 70,000 men. He had about half that number. Slipping in between the Austrians and Sardinians he defeated the former, notably at Dego, and drove them eastward. Then he turned westward against the Sardinians, defeated them at Mondovi and opened the way to Turin, their capital. The Sardinians sued for peace and agreed that France should have the provinces of Savoy and Nice. One enemy had thus been eliminated by the "rag heroes," now turned into "winged victories." Bonaparte summarized these achievements in a bulletin to his men, which set them vibrating. "Soldiers," he said, "in fifteen days you have won six victories, taken twenty-one stand of colors, fifty-five pieces of cannon, and several fortresses, and conquered the richest part of Piedmont. You have taken 1,500 prisoners and killed or wounded 10,000 men... . But, soldiers, you have done nothing, since there remains something for you to do. You have still battles to fight, towns to take, rivers to cross."

Bonaparte now turned his entire attention to the Austrians, who were in control of Lombardy. Rushing down the southern bank of the Po, he crossed it at Piacenza. Beaulieu, the Austrian commander, withdrew beyond the Adda River. There was no way to get at him but to cross the river by the bridge of Lodi, a bridge 350 feet long and swept on the other side by cannon. To cross it in the face of a raking fire was necessary but was well-nigh impossible. Bonaparte ordered his grenadiers forward. Halfway over they were mowed down by the Austrian fire and began to recoil. Bonaparte and other generals rushed to the head of the columns, risked their lives, inspired their men, and the result was that they got across in the very teeth of the murderous fire and seized the Austrian batteries. "Of all the actions in which the soldiers under my command have been engaged," reported Bonaparte to the Directory, "none has equaled the tremendous passage of the bridge of Lodi."

From that day Bonaparte was the idol of his soldiers. He had shown reckless courage, contempt of death. Thenceforth they called him affectionately "The Little Corporal." The Austrians retreated to the farther side of the Mincio and to the mighty fortress of Mantua. On May 16 Bonaparte made a triumphal entry into Milan. He sent a force to begin the siege of Mantua. That was the key to the situation. He could not advance into the Alps and against Vienna until he had taken it. On the other hand if Austria lost Mantua, she would lose her hold upon Italy.

Four times during the next eight months, from June, 1796, to January, 1797, Austria sent down armies from the Alps in the attempt to relieve the beleaguered fortress. Each time they were defeated, by the prodigious activity, the precision of aim, of the French general, who continued his policy of attacking his enemy piecemeal, before their divisions could unite. By this policy his inferior forces, for his numbers were inferior to the total of the opposed army, were always as a matter of fact so applied as to be superior to the enemy on the battlefield, for he attacked when the enemy was divided. It was youth against age, Bonaparte being twenty-seven, Wurmser and the other Austrian generals almost seventy. It was new methods against old, originality against the spirit of routine. The Austrians came down from the Alpine passes in two divisions. Here was Bonaparte's chance, and wonderfully did he use it. In war, said Moreau to him two years later, "the greater number always beat the lesser." "You are right," replied Bonaparte. "Whenever, with smaller forces I was in the presence of a great army, arranging mine rapidly, I fell like a thunderbolt upon one of its wings, tumbled it over, profited by the disorder which always ensued to attack the enemy elsewhere, always with my entire force. Thus I defeated him in detail and victory was always the triumph of the larger number over the smaller." All this was accomplished only by forced marches. "It is our legs that win his battles," said his soldiers. He shot his troops back and forth like a shuttle. By the rapidity of his movements he made up for his numerical weakness. Of course this success was rendered possible by the mistake of his opponents in dividing their forces when they should have kept them united.

Even thus, with his own ability and the mistakes of his enemies cooperating, the contest was severe, the outcome at times trembled in the balance. Thus at Arcola, the battle raged for three days. Again, as at Lodi, success depended upon the control of a bridge. Only a few miles separated the two Austrian divisions. If the Austrians could hold the bridge, then their junction could probably be completed. Bonaparte seized a flag and rushed upon the bridge, accompanied by his staff. The Austrians leveled a murderous fire at them. The columns fell back, several officers having been shot down. They refused to desert their general, but dragged him with them by his arms and clothes. He fell into a morass and began to sink. "Forward to save the General!" was the cry and immediately the French fury broke loose, they drove back the Austrians and rescued their hero. He had, however, not repeated the exploit of Lodi. He had not crossed the bridge. But the next day his army was victorious and the Austrians retreated once more. The three days' battle was over (November 15-17, 1796).

Two months later a new Austrian army came down from the Alps for the relief of Mantua and another desperate battle occurred, at Rivoli. On January 13-14, 1797, Bonaparte inflicted a crushing defeat upon the Austrians, routed them, and sent them spinning back into the Alps again. Two weeks later Mantua surrendered. Bonaparte now marched up into the Alps, constantly outgeneraling his brilliant new opponent, the young Archduke Charles, forcing him steadily back. When on April 7 he reached the little town of Leoben, about 100 miles from Vienna, Austria sued for peace. A memorable and crowded year of effort was thus brought to a brilliant close. In its twelve months' march across northern Italy the French had fought eighteen big battles, and sixty-five smaller ones. "You have, besides that," said Bonaparte in a bulletin to the army, "sent 30,000,000 from the public treasury to Paris. You have enriched the Museum of Paris with 300 masterpieces of ancient and modern Italy, which it has taken thirty ages to produce. You have conquered the most beautiful country of Europe. The French colors float for the first time upon the borders of the Adriatic." In another proclamation he told them they were forever covered with glory, that when they had completed their task and returned to their homes their fellow citizens, when pointing to them would say, "He was of the Army of Italy."

Thus rose his star to full meridian splendor. No wonder he believed in it.

All through this Italian campaign Bonaparte acted as if he were the head of the state, not its servant. He sometimes followed the advice of the Directors, more often he ignored it, frequently he acted in defiance of it. Military matters did not alone occupy his attention. He tried his hand at political manipulation, with the same confidence and the same success which he had shown on the field of battle. He became a creator and a destroyer of states. Italy was not at that time a united country but was a collection of small, independent states. None of these escaped the transforming touch of the young conqueror. He changed the old aristocratic republic of Genoa into the Ligurian Republic, giving it a constitution similar to that of France. He forced doubtful princes, like the Dukes of Parma and Modena, to submission and heavy payments. He forced the Pope to a similar humiliation, taking some of his states, sparing most of them, and levying heavy exactions.

His most notorious act, next to the conquest of the successive Austrian armies, was the overthrow, on a flimsy pretext and with diabolic guile, of the famous old Republic of Venice.

> *"Once did she hold the gorgeous East in fee;*
> *And was the safeguard of the West: the worth*
> *Of Venice did not fall below her birth,*
> *Venice, the Eldest Child of Liberty."*

Such was the thought that came to the poet Wordsworth as he contemplated this outrage, resembling in abysmal immorality the contemporary partition of Poland at the hands of the monarchs of Prussia, Austria, and Russia. At least this clear, bright, pagan republican general could have claimed, had he cared to, that he was no worse than the kings of the eighteenth century who asserted that their rule was ordained of God. Bonaparte was no worse; he was also no better; he was, moreover, far more able. He conquered Venice, one of the oldest and proudest states in Europe, and held it as a pawn in the game of diplomacy, to which he turned with eagerness and talent, now that the war was over.

Austria had agreed in April, 1797, to the preliminary peace of Leoben. The following summer was devoted to the making of the final peace, that of Campo Formio, concluded October 17, 1797. During these months Bonaparte lived in state in the splendid villa of Montebello, near Milan, basking in the dazzling sunshine of his sudden and amazing fortune. There he kept a veritable court, receiving ambassadors, talking intimately with artists and men of letters, surrounded by young officers, who had caught the swift contagion of his personality and who were advancing with his advance to prosperity and renown. There, too, at Montebello, were Josephine and the brothers and the sisters of the young victor and also his mother, who kept a level head in prosperity as she had in adversity — all irradiated with the new glamour of their changed position in life. The young man who a few years before had pawned his watch and had eaten six-cent dinners in cheap Parisian restaurants now dined in public in the old manner of French kings, allowing the curious to gaze upon him. A bodyguard of Polish lancers attended whenever he rode forth.

His conversation dazzled by its ease and richness. It was quoted everywhere. Some of it was calculated to arouse concern in high quarters. "What I have done so far," he said, "is nothing. I am but at the beginning of the career I am to run. Do you imagine that I have triumphed in Italy in order to advance the lawyers of the Directory? … Let the Directory attempt to deprive me of my command and they will see who is the master. The nation must have a head who is rendered illustrious by glory." Two years later he saw to it that she had such a head.

The treaty of Campo Formio initiated the process of changing the map of Europe which was to be carried on bewilderingly in the years to come. Neither France, champion of the new principles of politics, nor Austria, champion of the old, differed in their methods. Both bargained and traded as best they could, and the result was an agreement that contravened the principles of the French Revolution, of the rights of peoples to determine their own destinies, the principle of popular sovereignty. For the agreement simply registered the arbitrament of the sword, was frankly based on force, and on nothing else. French domestic policy had been revolutionized. French foreign policy had remained stationary.

By the Treaty of Campo Formio Austria relinquished her possessions in Belgium to France and abandoned to her the left bank of the Rhine, agreeing to bring about a congress of the German states to effect this change. Austria also gave up her rights in Lombardy and agreed to recognize the new Cisalpine Republic which Bonaparte created out of Lombardy, the duchies of Parma and Modena, and out of parts of the Papal States and Venetia. In return for this the city, the islands, and most of the mainland of Venice, were handed over to Austria, as were also Dalmatia and Istria. Austria became an Adriatic power. The Adriatic ceased to be a Venetian lake.

The French people were enthusiastic over the acquisition of Belgium and the left bank of the Rhine. They were disposed, however, to be indignant at the treatment of Venice, the rape of a republic by a republic. But they were obliged to take the fly with the ointment and to adapt themselves to the situation. Thus ended the famous Italian campaign, which was the stepping-stone by which Napoleon Bonaparte started on his triumphal way.

He had, moreover, not only conquered Italy. He had plundered her. One of the features of this campaign had been that it had been based upon the principle that it must pay for itself and yield a profit in addition, for the French treasury. Bonaparte demanded large contributions from the princes whom he conquered. The Duke of Modena had to pay ten million francs, the republic of Genoa fifteen, the Pope twenty. He levied heavily upon Milan. Not only did he make Italy support his army but he sent large sums to the Directory, to meet the ever-threatening deficit.

Not only that, but he shamelessly and systematically robbed her of her works of art. This he made a regular feature of his career as conqueror. In this and later campaigns, whenever victorious, he had his agents ransack the galleries and select the pictures, which he then demanded as the prize of war, conduct which greatly embittered the victims but produced pleasurable feelings in France. The entry of the first art treasures into Paris created great excitement. Enormous cars bearing pictures and statues, carefully packed, but labeled on the outside, rolled through the streets to the accompaniment of martial music, the waving of flags, and shouts of popular approval; "The Transfiguration" by Raphael; "The Christ" by Titian; the Apollo Belvedere, the Nine Muses, the Laocoon, the Venus de Medici.

During his career Bonaparte enriched the Museum of the Louvre with over a hundred and fifty paintings by Raphael, Rembrandt, Rubens, Titian, and Van Dyck, to mention only a few of the greater names. After his fall years later many of these were returned to their former owners. Yet many remained. The famous bronze horses of Venice, of which the Venetians had robbed Constantinople centuries before, as Constantinople had long before that robbed Rome, were transported to Paris after the conquest of Venice in 1797, were transported back to Venice after the overthrow of Napoleon and were put in place again, there to remain for a full 100 years, until the year 1915, when they were removed once more, this time by the Venetians themselves, for purposes of safety against the dangers of the Austrian war of that year.

After this swift revelation of genius in the Italian campaign the laureled hero returned to Paris, the cynosure of all eyes, the center of boundless curiosity. He knew, however, that the way to keep curiosity alive is not to satisfy it, for, once satisfied, it turns to other objects. Believing that the Parisians, like the ancient Athenians, preferred to worship gods that were unknown, he discreetly kept in the background, affected simplicity of dress and demeanor, and won praises for his "modesty," quite ironically misplaced. Modesty was not his forte. He was studying his future very carefully, was analyzing the situation very closely. He would have liked to enter the Directory. Once one of the five he could have pocketed the other four. But he was only twenty-eight and Directors must be at least forty years of age. He did not wish or intend to imitate Cincinnatus by returning with dignity to the plow. He was resolved to "keep his glory warm." Perceiving that, as he expressed it, "the pear was not yet ripe," he meditated, and the result of his meditations was a spectacular adventure.

After the Peace of Campo Formio only one power remained at war with France, namely England. But England was most formidable — because of her wealth, because of her colonies, because of her navy. She had been the center of the coalition, the pay-mistress of the other enemies, the constant fomenter of trouble, the patron of the Bourbons. "Our Government," said Napoleon at this time, "must destroy the English monarchy or it must expect itself to be destroyed by these active islanders. Let us concentrate our energies on the navy and annihilate England. That done, Europe is at our feet." The annihilation of England was to be the most constant subject of his thought during his entire career, baffling him at every stage, prompting him to gigantic efforts, ending in catastrophic failure eighteen years later at Waterloo, and in the forced repinings of St. Helena.

The Directory now made Bonaparte commander of the army of England, and he began his first experiment in the elusive art of destroying these "active islanders." Seeing that a direct invasion of England was impossible he sought out a vulnerable spot which should at the same time be accessible, and he hit upon Egypt. Not that Egypt was an English possession, for it was not. It belonged to the Sultan of Turkey. But it was on the route to India and Bonaparte, like many of his contemporaries, considered that England drew her strength, not from English mines and factories, from English brains and characters, but from the fabulous wealth of India. Once cut that nerve and the mighty colossus would reel and fall. England was not an island; she was a world-empire. As such she stood in the way of all other would-be world-empires, then as now. The year 1914 saw no new arguments put forth by her enemies in regard to England that were not freely uttered in 1797. Bonaparte denounced this "tyrant of the seas" quite in our latter-day style. If there must be tyranny it was intolerable that it should be exercised by others. He now received the ready sanction of the Directors to his plan for the conquest of Egypt. Once conquered, Egypt would serve as a basis of operations for an expedition to India which would come in time. The Directors were glad to get him so far away from Paris, where his popularity was burdensome, was, indeed, a constant menace. The plan itself, also, was quite in the traditions of the French foreign office. Moreover the potent fascination of the Orient for all imaginative minds, as offering an inviting, mysterious field for vast and dazzling action, operated powerfully upon Bonaparte. What destinies might not be carved out of the gorgeous East, with its limitless horizons, its immeasurable, unutilized opportunities? The Orient had appealed to Alexander the Great with irresistible force as it now appealed to this imaginative young Corsican, every energy of whose rich and complex personality was now in high flood. "This little Europe has not enough to offer," he remarked one day to his schoolboy friend, Bourrienne. "The Orient is the place to go to. All great reputations have been made there." "I do not know what would have happened to me," he said later, "if I had not had the happy idea of going to Egypt." He was a child of the Mediterranean and as a boy had drunk in its legends and its poetry. As wildly imaginative as he was intensely practical, both imagination and cool calculation recommended the adventure.

Once decided on, preparations were made with promptness and in utter secrecy. On May 19, 1798, Bonaparte set sail from Toulon with a fleet of 400 slow-moving transports bearing an army of 38,000 men. A brilliant corps of young generals accompanied him, Berthier, Murat, Desaix, Marmont, Lannes, Kleber, tried and tested in Italy the year before. He also took with him a traveling library in which Plutarch's Lives and Xenophon's Anabasis and the Koran were a few of the significant contents. Fellow-voyagers, also, were over 100 distinguished scholars, scientists, artists, engineers, for this expedition was to be no mere military promenade, but was designed to widen the bounds of human knowledge by an elaborate study of the products and customs, the history and the art of that country, famous, yet little known. This, indeed, was destined to be the most permanent and valuable result of an expedition which laid the broad foundations of modern Egyptology in "The Description of Egypt," a monumental work which presented to the world in sumptuous form the discoveries and investigations of this group of learned men.

The hazards were enormous. Admiral Nelson with a powerful English fleet was in the Mediterranean. The French managed to escape him. Stopping on the way to seize the important position of Malta and to forward the contents of its treasury to the Directors, Bonaparte reached his destination at the end of June and disembarked in safety. The nominal ruler of Egypt was the Sultan of Turkey, but the real rulers were the Mamelukes, a sort of feudal military caste. They constituted a splendid body of cavalrymen, but they were no match for the invaders, as they lacked infantry and artillery, and were, moreover, far inferior in numbers.

Seizing Alexandria on July 2 the French army began the march to Cairo. The difficulties of the march were great, as no account had been taken, in the preparations, of the character of the climate and the country. The soldiers wore the heavy uniforms in vogue in Europe. In the march across the blazing sands they experienced hunger, thirst, heat. Many perished from thirst, serious eye troubles were caused by the frightful glare, suicide was not infrequent. Finally, however, after nearly three weeks of this agony, the Pyramids came in sight, just outside Cairo. There Bonaparte administered a smashing defeat to the Mamelukes, encouraging his soldiers by one of his thrilling phrases, "Soldiers, from the summit of these pyramids forty centuries look down upon you." The Battle of the Pyramids, July 21, 1798, gave the French control of Cairo. The Mamelukes were dispersed. They had lost 2,000 men. Bonaparte had lost very few.

But no sooner had the French conquered the country than they became prisoners in it. For, on August 1 Nelson had surprised the French fleet as it was lying in the harbor of Abukir Bay, east of Alexandria, and had captured or destroyed it. Only two battleships and a frigate managed to escape. This Battle of the Nile, as it was called, was one of the most decisive sea fights of this entire period. It was Bonaparte's first taste of British sea power. It was not his last.

Bonaparte received the news of this terrible disaster, which cut him off from France and cooped him up in a hot and poor country, with superb composure. "Well! we must remain in this land, and come forth great, as did the ancients. This is the hour when characters of a superior order should show themselves." And later he said that the English "will perhaps compel us to do greater things than we intended."

He had need of all his resources, material and moral. Hearing that the Sultan of Turkey had declared war upon him, he resolved in January, 1799, to invade Syria, one of the Sultan's provinces, wishing to restore or reaffirm the confidence of his soldiers by fresh victories and thinking, perhaps, of a march on India or on Constantinople, taking "Europe in the rear," as he expressed it. If such was his hope, it was destined to disappointment. The crossing of the desert from Egypt into Syria was painful in the extreme, marked by the horrors of heat and thirst. The soldiers marched amid clouds of sand blown against them by a suffocating wind. They however seized the forts of Gaza and Jaffa, and destroyed a Turkish army at Mt. Tabor, near Nazareth, but were arrested at Acre, which they could not take by siege, because it was on the seacoast and was aided by the British fleet, but which they partly took by storm, only to be forced finally to withdraw because of terrific losses. For two months the struggle for Acre went on. Plague broke out, ammunition ran short, and Bonaparte was again beaten by sea power. He led his army back to Cairo in a memorable march, covering 300 miles in twenty-six days, over scorching sands and amidst appalling scenes of disaster and desperation. He had sacrificed 5,000 men, had accomplished nothing, and had been checked for the first time in his career. On reaching Cairo he had the effrontery to act as if he had been triumphant, and sent out lying bulletins, not caring to have the truth known.

A few weeks later he did win a notable victory, this time at Abukir, against a Turkish army that had just disembarked. This he correctly described when he announced, "It is one of the finest I have ever witnessed. Of the army landed by the enemy not a man has escaped." Over 10,000 Turks lost their lives in this, the last exploit of Bonaparte in Egypt. For now he resolved to return to France, to leave the whole adventure in other hands, seeing that it must inevitably fail, and to seek his fortune in fairer fields. He had heard news from France that made him anxious to return. A new coalition had been formed during his absence, the French had been driven out of Italy, France itself was threatened with invasion. The Directory was discredited and unpopular because of its incompetence and blunders. Bonaparte did not dare inform his soldiers, who had endured so much, of his plan. He did not even dare to tell Kleber, to whom he entrusted the command of the army by a letter which reached the latter too late for him to protest. He set sail secretly on the night of August 21, 1799, accompanied by Berthier, Murat, and five other officers and by two or three scientists. Kleber was later assassinated by a Mohammedan fanatic and the French army was forced to capitulate and evacuate Egypt, in August, 1801. That ended the Egyptian expedition.

It was no easy thing to get back from Egypt to France with the English scouring the seas and the winds against him. Sometimes the little sail-boat on which Bonaparte had taken passage was beaten back ten miles a day. Then the wind would shift at night and progress would be made. It took three weeks of hugging the southern shore of the Mediterranean before the narrows between Africa and Sicily were reached. These were guarded by an English battleship. But the French slipped through at night, lights out. Reaching Corsica they stopped several days, the winds dead against them. It seemed as if everyone on the island claimed relationship with their fellow citizen who had been rendered "illustrious by glory." Bonaparte saw his native land for the last time in his life. Finally he sailed for France, and was nearly overhauled by the British, who chased him to almost within sight of land. The journey from the coast to Paris was a continuous ovation. The crowds were such that frequently the carriages could advance but slowly. Evenings there were illuminations everywhere. When Paris was reached delirium broke forth.

He arrived in the nick of time, as was his wont. Finally the pear was ripe. The government was in the last stages of unpopularity and discredit. Incompetent and corrupt, it was also unsuccessful. The Directory was in existence for four years, from October, 1795, to November, 1799. Its career was agitated. The defects of the constitution, the perplexing circumstances of the times, the ambitions and intrigues of individuals, seeking personal advantage and recking little of the state, had strained the institutions of the country almost to the breaking point, and had created a widespread feeling of weariness and disgust. Friction had been constant between the Directors and the legislature, and on two occasions the former had laid violent hands upon the latter, once arresting a group of royalist deputies and annulling their election, once doing the same to a group of radical republicans. They had thus made sport of the constitution and destroyed the rights of the voters. Their foreign policy, after Bonaparte had sailed for Egypt, had been so aggressive and blundering that a new coalition had been formed against France, consisting of England, Austria, and Russia, which country now abandoned its eastern isolation and entered upon a period of active participation in the affairs of western Europe. The coalition was successful, the French were driven out of Germany back upon the Rhine, out of Italy, and the invasion of France was, perhaps, impending. The domestic policy of the Directors had also resulted in fanning once more the embers of religious war in Vendee.

In these troubled waters Bonaparte began forthwith to fish. He established connections with a group of politicians who for one reason and another considered a revision of the constitution desirable and necessary. The leader of the group was Sieyes, a man who plumed himself on having a complete knowledge of the art and theory of government and who now wished to endow France with the perfect institutions of which he carried the secret in his brain. Sieyes was a man of Olympian conceit, of oracular utterances, a coiner of telling phrases, enjoying an immoderate reputation as a constitution-maker. His phrase was now that to accomplish the desired change he needed "a sword." He would furnish the pen himself. The event was to prove, contrary to all proverbs, that the pen is weaker than the sword, at least when the latter belongs to a Napoleon Bonaparte. Bonaparte, who really despised "this cunning priest," as he called him, was nevertheless quite willing to use him as a stepping-stone. Heaping flatteries upon him he said: "We have no government, because we have no constitution; at least not the one we need. It is for your genius to give us one."

The plan these and other conspirators worked out was to force the Directors to resign, willy-nilly, thus leaving France without an executive, a situation that could not possibly be permitted to continue; then to get the Council of Elders and the Council of the Five Hundred to appoint a committee to revise the constitution. Naturally Sieyes and Bonaparte were to be on that committee, if all went well. Then let wisdom have her sway. The conspirators had two of the Directors on their side and a majority of the Elders, and fortunately the President of the Council of Five Hundred was a brother of Napoleon, Lucien

Bonaparte, a shallow but cool-headed rhetorician, to whom the honors of the critical day were destined to be due.

Thus was plotted in the dark the coup d'état of Brumaire which landed Napoleon in the saddle, made him ruler of a great state, and opened a new and prodigious chapter in the history of Europe. There is no English word for coup d'état, as fortunately the thing described is alien to the history of English-speaking peoples. It is the seizure of the state, of power, by force and ruse, the overthrow of the form of government by violence, by arms. There had been coups d'état before in France. There were to be others later, in the nineteenth century. But the coup d'état of 18th and 19th Brumaire (November 9 and 10, 1799) is the most classical example of this device, the most successful, the most momentous in its consequences.

But how to set the artful scheme in motion? There was the danger that the deputies of the Five Hundred might block the way, danger of a popular insurrection in Paris of the old familiar kind, if the rumor got abroad that the Republic was in peril. The conspirators must step warily. They did so — and they nearly failed — and had they failed, their fate would have been that of Robespierre.

A charge was trumped up, for which no evidence was given, that a plot was being concerted against the Republic. Not an instant must be lost, if the state was to be saved. The Council of Elders, informed of this, and already won over to the conspiracy, thereupon voted, upon the 18th of Brumaire, that both Councils should meet the following day at St. Cloud, several miles from Paris, and that General Bonaparte should take command of the troops for the purpose of protecting them.

The next day, Sunday, the two Councils met in the palace of St. Cloud. Delay occurring in arranging the halls for the extraordinary meeting, the suspicious legislators had time to confer, to concert opposition. The Elders, when their session finally began at two o'clock, demanded details concerning the pretended plot. Bonaparte entered and made a wild and incoherent speech. They were "standing on a volcano," he told them. He was no "Caesar" or "Cromwell" intent upon destroying the liberties of his country. "General, you no longer know what you are saying," whispered Bourrienne, urging him to leave the chamber, which he immediately did.

This was a bad beginning; but worse was yet to come. Bonaparte went to the Council of Five Hundred, accompanied by four grenadiers. He was greeted with a perfect storm of wrath. Cries of "Outlaw him, outlaw him!" "Down with the Dictator, down with the tyrant!" rent the air. Pandemonium reigned. He received blows, was pushed and jostled, and was finally dragged fainting from the hall by the grenadiers, his coat torn, his face bleeding. Outside he mounted his horse in the courtyard, before the soldiers.

It was Lucien who saved this badly bungled day. Refusing to put the motion to outlaw his brother, he left the chair, made his way to the courtyard, mounted a horse and harangued the soldiers, telling them that a band of assassins was terrorizing the Assembly, that his life and that of Napoleon were no longer safe, and demanding, as President of the Five Hundred, that the soldiers enter the hall and clear out the brigands and free the Council. The soldiers hesitated. Then Lucien seized Napoleon's sword, pointed it at his brother's breast, and swore to kill him if he should ever lay violent hands on the Republic. The lie and the melodrama worked. The soldiers entered the hall, led by Murat. The legislators escaped through the windows.

That evening groups of Elders and of the Five Hundred who favored the conspirators met, voted the abolition of the Directory, and appointed three Consuls, Sieyes, Ducos, and General Bonaparte, to take their place. They then adjourned for four months, appointing, as their final act, committees to cooperate with the Consuls in the preparation of a new constitution, rendered necessary by the changed conditions.

The three Consuls promised "fidelity to the Republic, one and indivisible, to liberty, equality, and the representative system of government." At six o'clock on Monday morning everyone went back to Paris. The grenadiers returned to their garrison singing revolutionary songs and thinking most sincerely that they had saved the Republic and the Revolution. No outbreak occurred in Paris. The coup d'état was popular. Government bonds rose rapidly, nearly doubling in a week.

Such was the Little Corporal's rise to civil power. It was fortunate, as we have seen, that not all the ability of his remarkable family was monopolized by himself. Lucien had his particular share, a distinct advantage to his kith and kin.

# CHAPTER VII

## THE CONSULATE

THUS the famous young warrior had clutched at power and was not soon to let it slip. It had been a narrow escape. Fate had trembled dangerously in the balance on that gray November Sunday afternoon, but the gambler had won. His thin, sallow face, his sharp, metallic voice, his abrupt, imperious gesture, his glance that cowed and terrified, his long disordered hair, his delicate hands, became a part of the history of the times, manifesting the intensely vivid impression which he had made upon his age and was to deepen. He was to etch the impress of his amazing personality with deep, precise, bold strokes upon the institutions and the life of France.

He was, in reality, a flinty young despot with a pronounced taste for military glory. "I love power," he said later, "as a musician loves his violin. I love it as an artist." He was now in a position to indulge his taste.

Pending a wider and a higher flight, there were two tasks that called for the immediate attention of the three Consuls, who now took the place formerly occupied by the five Directors. A new constitution must be made, and the war against the coalition must be carried on.

The Constitution of the Year VIII (1799), the fourth since the beginning of the Revolution, hastily composed and put into force a month after the coup d'état, was in its essentials the work of Bonaparte and was designed to place supreme power in his hands. This had not been at all the purpose of Sieyes or of the committees appointed to draft the document. But Sieyes' plan, which had not been carefully worked out but was confused and uncertain in many particulars, encountered the abrupt disdain of Bonaparte. There was to be a Grand Elector with a palace at Versailles and an income of six million francs a year. This was the place evidently intended for Bonaparte, who immediately killed it with the statement that he had no desire to be merely "a fatted pig." Impatient with this scheme and with others suggested by the committees, Bonaparte practically dictated the constitution, using, to be sure, such of the suggestions made by the others as seemed to him good or harmless. The result was the organization of that phase of the history of the Republic which is called the Consulate and which lasted from 1799 to 1804.

The executive power was vested in three Consuls who were to be elected for ten years and to be reeligible. They were to be elected by the Senate, but, to get the system started, the constitution indicated who they should be — Bonaparte, First Consul; Cambaceres, the second, and Lebrun, the third. Practically all the powers were to be in the hands of the First Consul, the appointment of ministers, ambassadors, officers of the army and navy, and numberless civil officials, including judges, the right to make war and peace, and treaties, subject to the sanction of the Legislature.

The First Consul was also to have the initiative in all legislation. Bills were to be prepared by a Council of State, were then to be submitted to a body called the Tribunate, which was to have the right to discuss them but not to vote them. Then they were to go to the Legislative Body, which was to have the power to vote them but not discuss them. Moreover this "assembly of 300 mutes" must discharge its single function of voting in secret. There was also to be a fourth body, higher than the others — the Senate, which was to be the guardian of the constitution and was also to be an electing body, choosing the Consuls, the members of the Tribunate and the Legislature from certain lists, prepared in a cumbersome and elaborate way, and pretending to safeguard the right of the voters, for the suffrage was declared by the constitution to be universal. No time need be spent on this aspect of the constitution, for it was a sham and a deception.

All this elaborate machinery was designed to keep up the fiction of the sovereignty of the people, the great assertion of the Revolution. The Republic continued to exist. The people were voters. They had their various assemblies, thus ingeniously selected. Practically, however, and this is the matter that most concerns us, popular sovereignty was gone, Bonaparte was sovereign. He had more extensive executive powers than Louis XVI had had under the Constitution of 1791. He really had the legislative power also. No bill could be discussed or voted that had not been first prepared by his orders. Once voted it could not go into force until he promulgated it. France was still a republic in name; practically, however, it was a monarchy, scarcely veiled at that. Bonaparte's position was quite as attractive as that of any monarch by divine right, except for the fact that he was to hold it for a term of ten years only and had no power to bequeath it to an heir. He was to remedy these details later.

Having given France a constitution, he secured the enactment of a law which placed all the local government in his hands. There was to be a prefect at the head of each department, a sub-prefect for a smaller division, a mayor for every town or commune. The citizens lost the power to manage their own local affairs, and thus their training in self-government came to an end. Government, national and local, was centralized in Paris, more effectively, even, than in the good old days of the Bourbons and their intendants.

Having set his house in order, having gained a firm grip on the reins of power, Bonaparte now turned his attention to the foreign enemies of France. The coalition consisted of England, Austria, and Russia. England was difficult to get at. The Russians were dissatisfied with their allies and were withdrawing from cooperation. There remained Austria, the enemy Bonaparte had met before.

One Austrian army was on the Rhine and Bonaparte sent Moreau to attack it. Another was in northern Italy and he went in person to attend to that. While he had been in Egypt the Austrians had won back northern Italy. Melas, their general, had driven Massena into Genoa, where the latter hung on like grim death, with rations that would soon be exhausted. Bonaparte's plan was to get in between the Austrians and their own country, to attack them in the rear, thus to force them to withdraw from the siege of Genoa in order to keep open their line of communication. In the pursuit of this object he accomplished one of his most famous exploits, the crossing of the Great Saint Bernard pass over the Alps, with an army of 40,000, through snow and ice, dragging their cannon in troughs made out of hollowed logs. It was a matter of a week. Once in Italy he sought out the Austrians and met them unexpectedly at Marengo (June 14, 1800). The battle came near being a defeat, owing to the fact that Bonaparte blundered badly, having divided his forces, and that Desaix's division was miles away. The battle began at dawn and went disastrously for the French. At one o'clock the Austrian commander rode back to his headquarters, believing that he had won and that the remaining work could be left to his subordinates. The French were pushed back and their retreat threatened to become a stampede. The day was saved by the appearance of Desaix's division on the scene, at about five o'clock. The battle was resumed with fury, Desaix himself was killed, but the soldiers avenged his glorious death by a glorious victory. By seven o'clock the day of strange vicissitudes was over. The Austrians signed an armistice abandoning to the French all northern Italy as far as the Mincio.

Six months later Moreau won a decisive victory over the Austrians in Germany at Hohenlinden (December 3, 1800), thus opening the road to Vienna. Austria was now compelled to sue for peace. The Treaty of Luneville (February 9, 1801) was in the main a repetition of the Treaty of Campo Formio.

As had been the case after Campo Formio, so now, after the break-up of this second coalition, France remained at war with only one nation, England. These two nations had been at war continuously for eight years. England had defeated the French navy and had conquered many of the colonies of France and of the allies or dependencies of France, that is, of Holland and Spain. She had just compelled the French in Egypt, the army left there by Bonaparte, to agree to evacuate that country. But her debt had grown enormously and there was widespread popular dislike of the war. A change in the ministry occurred, removing the great war leader, William Pitt. England agreed to discuss the question of peace. The discussion went on for five months and ended in the Peace of Amiens (March, 1802). England recognized the existence of the French Republic. She restored all the French colonies and some of the Dutch and

Spanish, retaining only Ceylon and Trinidad. She promised to evacuate Malta and Egypt, which the French had seized in 1798 and which she had taken from them. Nothing was said of the French conquest of Belgium and the left bank of the Rhine. This was virtually acquiescence in the new boundaries of France, which far exceeded those of the ancient monarchy.

Thus Europe was at peace for the first time in ten years. Great was the enthusiasm in both France and England.

The peace, however, was most unstable. It lasted just one year.

Napoleon said on one occasion, "I am the Revolution." On another he said that he had "destroyed the Revolution." There was much error and some truth in both these statements.

The Consulate, and the Empire which succeeded the Consulate, preserved much of the work of the Revolution and abolished much, in conformity with the ideas and also the personal interests of the new ruler. Bonaparte had very definite opinions concerning the Revolution, concerning the French people, and concerning his own ambitions. These opinions constituted the most important single factor in the life of France after 1799. Bonaparte sympathized with, or at least tolerated, one of the ideas of the Revolution, Equality. He detested the other leading idea, Liberty. In his youth he had fallen under the magnetic spell of Rousseau. But that had passed and thenceforth he dismissed Rousseau summarily as a "madman." He accepted the principle of equality because it alone made possible his own career and because he perceived the hold it had upon the minds of the people. He had no desire to restore the Bourbons and the feudal system, the incarnation of the principle of inequality and privilege. He stood right athwart the road to yesterday in this respect. It was he and his system that kept the Bourbons exiles from France fifteen years longer, so long indeed that when they did finally return it was largely without their baggage of outworn ideas. Bonaparte thus prevented the restoration of the Old Regime. That was done for, for good and all. Privilege, abolished in 1789, remained abolished. The clergy, nobility, and third estate had been swept away. There remained only a vast mass of French citizens subject to the same laws, paying the same taxes, enjoying equal chances in life, as far as the state was concerned. The state showed no partiality, had no favorites. All shared in bearing the nation's burdens in proportion to their ability. And no class levied taxes upon another — tithes and feudal dues were not restored. No class could exercise a monopoly of any craft or trade — the guilds with all their restrictions remained abolished. Moreover all now had an equal chance at public employment in the state or in the army.

Bonaparte summed this policy up in the phrase "careers open to talent." This idea was not original with him, it was contained in the Declaration of the Rights of Man. But he held it. Under him there were no artificial barriers, any one might rise as high as his ability, his industry, his service justified, always on condition of his loyalty to the sovereign. Every avenue was kept open to ambition and energy. Napoleon's marshals, the men who attained the highest positions in his armies, were humbly born — Massena was the son of a saloon-keeper, Augereau of a mason, Ney of a cooper, and Murat of a country inn-keeper. None of these men could have possibly become a marshal under the Old Regime, nor could Bonaparte himself possibly ever have risen to a higher rank than that of colonel and then only when well along in life. Bonaparte did not think that all men are equal in natural gifts or in social position, but he maintained equality before the law, that priceless acquisition of the Revolution.

He did not believe in liberty nor did he believe that, for that matter, the French believed in it. His career was one long denial or negation of it. Neither liberty of speech, nor liberty of the press, neither intellectual nor political liberty, received anything from him but blows and infringements. In this respect his rule meant reaction to the spirit and the practice of the Old Regime. It is quite true that the Convention and the Directory had also trampled ruthlessly upon this principle, but it is also quite true that neither he nor they could successfully defy what is plainly a dominant preoccupation, a deep-seated longing of the modern world. For the last hundred years the ground has been cumbered with those who thought they could silence this passion for freedom, and who found out, to their cost and the cost of others, that their efforts to imprison the human spirit were unavailing. There are still, after all these instructive hundred years, rulers who share that opinion and act upon it. They have been able to preserve themselves and their methods of government in certain countries. But their day of reckoning, it may safely be prophesied, is coming, as it came for Napoleon himself. They fight for a losing cause, as the history of the modern world shows.

The activities of Bonaparte as First Consul, after Marengo and during the brief interval of peace, were unremitting and far-reaching. It was then that he gave his full measure as a civil ruler. He was concerned with binding up the wounds or open sores of the nation, with determining the precise form of the national institutions, with fashioning the mould through which the national life was to go pulsing for a long future, with consolidating the foundations of his power. A brief examination of this phase of his activity is essential to a knowledge of the later history of France, and to our appreciation of his own matchless and varied ability, of the power of sheer intellect and will applied to the problems of a society in flux.

First, the party passions which had rioted for ten years must be quieted. Bonaparte's policy toward the factions was conciliation, coupled with stern and even savage repression of such elements as refused to comply with this primary requirement. There was room enough in France for all, but on one condition, that all accept the present rulers and acquiesce in the existing institutions and laws of the land. Offices would be open freely to former royalists, Jacobins, Girondists, on equal terms, no questions asked save that of loyalty. As a matter of fact Bonaparte exercised his vast appointing power in this sense for the purpose of effacing all distinctions, all unhappy reminders of a troubled past. The laws against the emigres and the recalcitrant priests were relaxed. Of over 100,000 emigrants, all but about 1,000 irreconcilables received, by successive decrees, the legal right to return and to recover their estates, if these had not been already sold. Only those who placed their devotion to the House of Bourbon above all other considerations found the door resolutely closed.

Bonaparte soon perceived that the strength of the Bourbon cause lay not in the merits or talents of the royal family itself or its aristocratic supporters, but in its close identification with the authorities of the Roman Catholic Church. Through all the angry religious warfare of the Revolution the mass of the people had remained faithful to the priests and the priests were subject to the bishops. The bishops had refused to accept the various laws of the Revolution concerning them and had as a consequence been driven from the country. They were living mostly in England and in Germany, taking their cue from the Pope, who recognized Louis XVIII, brother of Louis XVI, as the legitimate ruler of France.

Thus the religious dissension was fused with political opposition — royalists and bishops were in the same galley. Bonaparte determined to sever this connection, thus leaving the extreme royalists high and dry, a staff of officers without an army. No sooner had he returned from Marengo than he took measures to show the Catholics that they had nothing to fear from him, that they could enjoy their religion undisturbed if they did not use their liberty, under cover of religion, to plot against him and against the Revolutionary settlement. He was in all this not actuated by any religious sentiment himself, but by a purely political sentiment — he was himself, as he said, "Mohammedan in Egypt, Catholic in France," not because he considered that either was in the exclusive or authentic possession of the truth, but because he was a man of sense who saw the futility of trying to dragoon by force men who were religious into any other camp than the one to which they naturally belonged. Bonaparte also saw that religion was an instrument which he might much better have on his side than allow to be on the side of his enemies. He looked on religion as a force in politics, nothing else. Purely political, not spiritual, considerations determined his policy in now concluding with the Pope the famous treaty or Concordat, which reversed much of the work of the Revolutionary assemblies, and determined the relations of church and state in France for the whole nineteenth century. This important piece of legislation of the year 1802 lasted 103 years, being abrogated only under the present republic, in 1905.

Bonaparte's thought was that by restoring the Catholic Church to something like its former primacy he would weaken the royalists. The people must have a religion, he said, but the religion must be in the hands of the government. Many of his adherents did not agree at all with him in this attitude. They thought it far wiser to keep church and state divorced as they had been by the latest legislation of the Revolution. Bonaparte discussed the matter with the famous philosopher Volney, whom he had just appointed a senator, saying to him, "France desires a religion." Volney replied that France also desired the Bourbons. At this Bonaparte assaulted the philosopher and gave him such a kick that he fell and lost consciousness. The army officers who were anti-clerical were bitter in their opposition and jibes, but Bonaparte went resolutely ahead. He knew the influence that priests exercise over their flocks and he intended that they should exercise it in his behalf. He meant to control them as he controlled the army and the thousands of state officials. The control of religion ought to be vested in the ruler. "It is impossible to govern without it," he said. He therefore turned to the Pope and made the treaty. "If the Pope had not existed," he said, "I should have had to create him for this occasion."

By the Concordat the Catholic religion was recognized by the Republic to be that "of the great majority of the French people" and its free exercise was permitted. The Pope agreed to a reorganization involving a diminution in the number of bishoprics. He also recognized the sale of the church property effected by the Revolution. Henceforth the bishops were to be appointed by the First Consul but were to be actually invested by the Pope. The bishops in turn were to appoint the priests, with the consent of the government. The bishops must take the oath of fidelity to the head of the state. Both bishops and priests were to receive salaries from the state. They really became state officials.

The Concordat gave great satisfaction to the mass of the population for two reasons — it gave them back the normal exercise of the religion in which they believed, and it confirmed their titles to the lands of the church which they had bought during the Revolution, titles which the church now recognized as legal. The church soon found that Bonaparte regarded it as merely another source of influence, an instrument of rule. The clergy now became his supporters and in large measure abandoned royalism. Moreover Bonaparte, by additional regulations to which he did not ask the Pope's assent, bound the clergy hand and foot to his own chariot.

The Concordat was nevertheless a mistake. France had worked out a policy of entire separation of church and state which, had it been allowed to continue, would have brought the blessing of toleration into the habits of the country. But the Concordat cut this promising development short and by tying church and state together in a union which each shortly found disagreeable it left to the entire nineteenth century an irritating and a dangerous problem. Nor did it preserve, for long, happy relations between Napoleon and the Pope. Not many years later a quarrel arose between them which grew and grew until the Pope excommunicated Napoleon and Napoleon seized the Pope and kept him prisoner. Napoleon himself came to consider the Concordat as the worst blunder in his career. However, its immediate advantages were considerable.

"My real glory," said Napoleon at St. Helena, "is not my having won forty battles. What will never be effaced, what will endure forever, is my Civil Code." He was undoubtedly mistaken as to the durability of this achievement, but he was correct in placing it higher than that activity which occupied far more of his time. The famous Code Napoleon was an orderly, systematic, compact statement of the laws of France. Pre-revolutionary France had been governed by a perplexing number of systems of law of different historical origins. Then had come, with the Revolution, a flood of new legislation, inspired by different principles and greatly increasing the sum-total of laws in force. It was desirable to sift and harmonize all these statutes, and to present to the people of France a body of law, clear, rational, and logically arranged, so that henceforth all the doubt, uncertainty, and confusion which had hitherto characterized the administration of justice might be avoided and every Frenchman might easily know what his legal rights and relations were, with reference to the state and his fellow-citizens. The Constituent Assembly, the Convention, the Directory, had all appreciated the need of this codification and had had committees at work upon it, but the work had been uncompleted. Bonaparte now lent the driving force of his personality to the accomplishment of this task, and in a comparatively brief time the lawyers and the Council of State to whom he intrusted the work had it finished. The code to which Napoleon attached his name preserved the principle of civil equality established by the Revolution. It was immediately put into force in France and was later introduced into countries conquered or influenced by France, Belgium, the German territories west of the Rhine, and Italy.

Bonaparte's own direct share in this monumental work was considerable and significant. Though no lawyer himself, and with little technical knowledge of law, his marvelous intellectual ability, the precision, penetration, and pertinence of many of his criticisms, suggestions, questions, gave color and tone and character to the completed work. He presided over many of the sessions of the Council of State devoted to the elaboration of this code. "He spoke," says a witness, "without embarrassment and without pretension. He was never inferior to any member of the Council; he often equaled the ablest of them by the ease with which he seized the point of a question, by the justness of his ideas and the force of his reasoning; he often surprised them by the turn of his phrases and the originality of his expression." Called a new Constantine by the clergy for having made the Concordat, Bonaparte was considered by the lawyers a new Justinian. He was as a matter of fact, in many respects, the superior of both.

During these years of the Consulate Bonaparte achieved many other things than those which have been mentioned. He improved the system of taxation greatly, and brought order into the national finances. He founded the Bank of France, which still exists — and another institution which has come down to our own day, the Legion of Honor, for the distribution of honors and emoluments to those who rendered distinguished service to the state. Opposed as un-democratic, as offensive to the principle of equality, it was nevertheless instituted. Though open to those who had rendered civil service as well as to those who had rendered military, as a matter of fact Napoleon conferred only 1,400 crosses out of 48,000 upon civilians.

Nor did this exhaust the list of durable achievements of this crowded period of the Consulate. The system of national education was in part reorganized, and industry and commerce received the interested attention of the ambitious ruler. Roads were improved, canals were cut, ports were dredged. The economic development of the country was so rapid as to occasion some uneasiness in England.

Thus was carried through an extensive and profound renovation of the national life. This period of the Consulate is that part of Bonaparte's career which was most useful to his fellow-men, most contributory to the welfare of his country. His work was not accomplished without risk to himself. As his reputation and authority increased, the wrath of those who saw their way to power barred by his formidable person increased also. At first the royalists had looked to him to imitate the English General Monk who had used his position for the restoration of Charles II. But Bonaparte had no notion of acting any such graceful and altruistic a part. When this became apparent certain reckless royalists commenced to plot against him, began considering that it was possible to murder him. An attack upon him occurred shortly after Marengo. Many lives were lost, but he escaped with his by the narrowest margin.

A more serious plot was woven in London in the circle of the Count of Artois, younger brother of Louis XVI. The principal agents were Georges Cadoudal and Pichegru. Bonaparte, through his police, knew of the plot. He hoped, in allowing it to develop, to get his hands on the Count of Artois. But the Count did not land in France. Cadoudal and his accomplices were taken and shot. Pichegru was found strangled in prison. Bonaparte wished to make an example of the House of Bourbon which would be remembered. This led him to commit a monstrous crime. He ordered the seizure on German soil of the young Duke d'Enghien, the Prince of Conde, a member of a branch of the Bourbon family. The prince, who was innocent of any connection whatever with the conspiracy, was abducted, brought to Vincennes at five o'clock on the evening of March 20, 1804, was sent before a court-martial at eleven o'clock and at half-past two in the night was taken out into the courtyard and shot. This was assassination pure and simple and it was Bonaparte's own act. It has remained ever since an odious blot upon his name, which the multitudinous seas cannot wash out. Its immediate object, however, was achieved. The royalists ceased plotting the murder of the Corsican.

A few days after this Bonaparte took another step forward in the consolidation of his powers. In 1802, after the Treaty of Amiens had been made, he had astutely contrived to have his consulate for ten years transformed into a consulate for life, with the right to name his successor. The only remaining step was taken in 1804 when a servile Senate approved a new constitution declaring him Emperor of the French, "this change being demanded by the interests of the French people." It was at any rate agreeable to the

French people, who in a popular vote or plebiscite ratified it overwhelmingly. Henceforth he is designated by his first name, in the manner of monarchs. It happened to be a more musical and sonorous name than most monarchs have possessed.

"I found the crown of France lying on the ground," Napoleon once said, "and I picked it up with my sword," a vivid summary of an important chapter in his biography.

# CHAPTER VIII

## THE EARLY YEARS OF THE EMPIRE

THE Empire lasted ten years, from 1804 to 1814. It was a period of uninterrupted warfare in which a long series of amazing victories was swallowed up in final, overwhelming defeat. The central, overmastering figure in this agitating story, dominating the decade so completely that it is known by his name, was this man whose ambition vaulted so dizzily, only to overleap itself. Napoleon ranks with Alexander, Caesar, Charlemagne, as one of the most powerful conquerors and rulers of history. It would be both interesting and instructive to compare these four. It is by no means certain that Napoleon would not be considered the greatest of them all. Certainly we have far more abundant information concerning him than we have concerning the others.

When he became emperor he was thirty-five years old and was in the full possession of all his magnificent powers. For he was marvelously gifted. His brain was a wonderful organ, swift in its processes, tenacious in its grip, lucid, precise, tireless, and it was served by an incredibly capacious and accurate memory. "He never blundered into victory," says Emerson, "but won his battles in his head, before he won them on the field." All his intellectual resources were available at any moment. He said of himself, "Different matters are stowed away in my brain as in a chest of drawers. When I wish to interrupt a piece of work I close that drawer and open another. None of them ever get mixed, never does this inconvenience or fatigue me. When I feel sleepy I shut all the drawers and go to sleep."

Napoleon possessed a varied and vivid imagination, was always, as he said, "living two years in advance," weaving plans and dreams and then considering coolly the necessary ways and means to realize them. This union of the practical and the poetic, the realistic and the imaginative, each raised to the highest pitch, was rendered potent by a will that recognized no obstacles, and by an almost superhuman activity. Napoleon loved work, and no man in Europe and few in all history have labored as did he. "Work is my element, for which I was born and fitted," he said at St. Helena, at the end of his life. "I have known the limits of the power of my arms and legs; I have never discovered those of my power of work." Working twelve or sixteen and, if necessary, twenty hours a day, rarely spending more than fifteen or twenty minutes at his meals, able to fall asleep at will, and to awaken with his mind instantly alert, he lost no time and drove his secretaries and subordinates at full speed. We gain some idea of the prodigious labor accomplished by him when we consider that his published correspondence, comprising 23,000 pieces, fills thirty-two volumes and that 50,000 additional letters dictated by him are known to be in existence but have not yet been printed. Here was no do-nothing king but the most industrious man in Europe. Happy, too, only in his work. The ordinary pleasures of men he found tedious, indulging in them only when his position rendered it necessary. He rarely smiled, he never laughed, his conversation was generally a monologue, but brilliant, animated, trenchant, rushing, frequently rude and impertinent. He had no scruples and he had no manners. He was ill-bred, as was shown in his relations with women, of whom he had a low opinion. His language, whether Italian or French, lacked distinction, finish, correctness, but never lacked saliency or interest. The Graces had not presided over his birth, but the Fates had. He had a magnificent talent as stage manager and actor, setting the scenes, playing the parts consummately in all the varied ceremonies in which he was necessarily involved, coronation, reviews, diplomatic audiences, interviews with other monarchs. His proclamations, his bulletins to his army were masterpieces. He could cajole in the silkiest tones, could threaten in the iciest, could shed tears or burst into violence, smashing furniture and bric-a-brac when he felt that such actions would produce the effect desired. The Pope, Pius VII, seeing him once in such a display of passion, observed, "tragedian," "comedian."

He had no friends, he despised all theorists like those who had sowed the fructifying seeds of the Revolution broadcast, he harried all opponents out of the country or into silence, he made his ministers mere hard-worked servants, but he won the admiration and devotion of his soldiers by the glamour of his victories, he held the peasantry in the hollow of his hand by constantly guaranteeing them their lands and their civil equality, the things which were, in their opinion, the only things in the Revolution that counted. He was as little as he was big. He would lie shamelessly, would cheat at cards, was superstitious in strange ways. He is a man of whom more evil and more good can be said and has been said than of many historical figures. He cannot be easily described, and certainly not in any brief compass.

Now that Napoleon was emperor he proceeded to organize the state imperially. Offices with high-sounding, ancient titles were created and filled. There was a Grand Chamberlain, a Grand Marshal of the Palace, a Grand Master of Ceremonies, and so on. A court was created, expensive, and as gay as it could be made to be at a soldier's orders. The Emperor's family, declared Princes of France, donned new titles and prepared for whatever honors and emoluments might flow from the bubbling fountain-head. The court resumed the manners and customs which had been in vogue before the Revolution. Republican simplicity gave way to imperial pretensions, attitudes, extravagances, pose. The constitution was revised to meet the situation, and Napoleon was crowned in a memorable and sumptuous ceremony in Notre Dame, the Pope coming all the way from Rome to assist — but not to crown. At the critical point in the splendid ceremony Napoleon crowned himself and then crowned the Empress. But the Pope poured the holy oil upon Napoleon's head. This former lieutenant of artillery thus became the "anointed of the Lord," in good though irregular standing. He crowned himself a little later King of Italy, after he had changed the Cisalpine Republic into the Kingdom of Italy (1805).

The history of the Empire is the history of ten years of uninterrupted war. Europe saw a universal menace to the independence and liberty of all states in the growing and arrogant ascendency of France, an ascendency and a threat all the more obvious and dangerous now that that country was absolutely in the hands of an autocrat, and that too an autocrat who had grown great by war and whose military tastes and talents would now have free rein. Napoleon was evoking on every occasion, intentionally and ostentatiously, the imperial souvenirs of Julius Caesar and of Charlemagne. What could this mean except that he planned to rule not only France, but Europe, consequently the world? Unless the other nations were willing to accept subordinate positions, were willing to abdicate their rank as equals in the family of nations, they must fight the dictatorship which was manifestly impending. Fundamentally this is what the ten years' war meant, the right of other states to live and prosper, not on mere sufferance of Napoleon, but by their own right and because universal domination or the undue ascendency of any single state would necessarily be dangerous to the other states and to whatever elements of civilization they represented. France already had that ascendency in 1804. Under Napoleon she made a tremendous effort to convert it into absolute and universal domination. She almost succeeded. That she failed was due primarily to the steadfast, unshakable opposition of one power, England, which never acquiesced in her pretensions, which fought them at every stage with all her might, through good report and through evil report, stirring up opposition wherever she could, weaving coalition after coalition, using her money and her navy untiringly in the effort. It was a war of the giants. A striking aspect of the matter was the struggle between sea-power, directed by England, and land-power, directed by Napoleon.

While the Empire was being organized in 1804 a new coalition was being formed against France, the third in the series we are studying. England and France had made peace at Amiens in 1802. That peace lasted only a year, until May 17, 1803. Then the two states flew to arms again. The reasons were various. England was jealous of the French expansion which had been secured by the treaties of Campo Formio and Luneville, French control of the left bank of the Rhine, French domination over considerable parts of the Italian peninsula, particularly French conquest of Belgium, including the fine port of Antwerp. England had always been opposed to French expansion, particularly northward along the Channel, which

Englishmen considered and called the English Channel. The English did not wish any rival along those shores. However, despite this, they had finally consented to make the Peace of Amiens. The chief motive was the condition of their industries. The long war, since 1793, had damaged their trade enormously. They hoped, by making peace with France, to find the markets of the Continent open to them once more, and thus to revive their trade. But they shortly saw that this was not at all the idea of France. Napoleon wished to develop the industries of France, wished to have French industries not only supply the French market but win the markets of the other countries on the Continent. He therefore established high protective tariffs with this end in view. Thus English competition was excluded or at least greatly reduced. The English were extremely angry and did not at all propose to lie down supinely, beaten without a struggle. That had never been their custom. War would be less burdensome, said their business men. For England commerce was her very breath of life. Without it she could not exist. This explains why, now that she entered upon a struggle in its defense, she did not lay down her arms again until she had her rival safely imprisoned in the island of St. Helena.

There were other causes of friction between the two countries which rendered peace most unstable. With both nations ready for war, though not eager for it, causes for rupture were not hard to find. War broke out between them in May, 1803. Napoleon immediately seized Hanover, a possession in Germany of the English king. He declared the long coast of Europe from Hanover southward and eastward to Taranto in Italy blockaded, that is, closed to English commerce, and he began to prepare for an invasion of England itself. This was a difficult task, requiring much time, for France was inferior to England on the seas, and yet, unless she could control the Channel for a while at least, she could not send an army of invasion. Napoleon established a vast camp of 150,000 men at Boulogne to be ready for the descent. He hastened the construction of hundreds of flat-boats for transport. Whether all this was mere make-believe intended to alarm England, whether he knew that after all it was a hopeless undertaking, and was simply displaying all this activity to compel England to think that peace would be wiser than running the risk of invasion, we do not positively know.

At any rate England was not intimidated. She prepared for defense, and she also prepared for offense by seeking and finding allies on the Continent, by building up a coalition which might hold Napoleon in check, which might, it was hoped, even drive France back within her original boundaries, taking away from her the recent acquisitions of Belgium, the left bank of the Rhine, and the Italian annexations and protectorates. England made a treaty to this effect with Russia, which had her own reasons for opposing France — her dread of his projects in the eastern Mediterranean at the expense of the Turkish Empire. For if anyone was to carve up the Turkish Empire Russia wished to do it herself. The English agreed to pay subsidies to the Czar, a certain amount for every 100,000 men she should furnish for the war.

Finally in 1805 Austria entered the coalition, jealous of Napoleon's aggressions in Italy, anxious to wipe out the memory of the defeats of the two campaigns in which he had conquered her in 1796 and 1800, eager, also, to recover the position she had once held as the dominant power in the Italian peninsula.

Such was the situation in 1805. When he was quite ready Napoleon struck with tremendous effect, not against England, which he could not reach because of the silver streak of sea that lay between them, not against Russia, which was too remote for immediate attention, but against his old-time enemy, Austria, and he bowled her over more summarily and more humiliatingly than he had ever done before.

The campaign of 1805 was another Napoleonic masterpiece. The Austrians, not waiting for their allies, the Russians, to come up, had sent an army of 80,000 men under General Mack up the Danube into Bavaria. Mack had taken his position at Ulm, expecting that Napoleon would come through the passes of the Black Forest, the most direct and the usual way for a French army invading southern Germany. But not at all. Napoleon had a very different plan. Sending enough troops into the Black Forest region to confirm Mack in his opinion that this was the strategic point to hold, and thus keeping him rooted there, Napoleon transferred his Grand Army from Boulogne and the shores of the English Channel, where it had been training for the past two years, across Germany from north to south, a distance of 500 miles, in twenty-three days of forced marches, conducted in astonishing secrecy and with mathematical precision. He thus threw himself into the rear of Mack's army, between it and Vienna, cutting the line of communication, and repeating the strategy of the Great Saint Bernard and Marengo campaign of 1800. Mack had expected Napoleon to come from the west through the Black Forest. Instead, when it was too late, he found him coming from the east, up the Danube, toward Ulm. Napoleon made short work of Mack, forcing him to capitulate at Ulm, October 20th. "I have accomplished what I set out to do," Napoleon wrote Josephine. "I have destroyed the Austrian army by means of marches alone." It was a victory won by legs — 60,000 prisoners, 120 guns, more than thirty generals. It had cost him only 1,500 men.

The way was now open down the Danube to Vienna. Thither, along poor roads and through rain and snow, Napoleon rushed, covering the distance in three weeks. Vienna was entered in triumph and without resistance, as the Emperor Francis had retired in a north-easterly direction, desiring to effect a junction with the oncoming Russian army. Napoleon followed him and on December 2, 1805, won perhaps his most famous victory, the battle of Austerlitz, on the first anniversary of his coronation as Emperor. All day long the battle raged. The sun breaking through the wintry fogs was considered a favorable omen by the French and henceforth became the legendary symbol of success. The fighting was terrific. The bravery of the soldiers on both sides was boundless, but the generalship of Napoleon was as superior as that of the Austro-Russians was faulty. The result was decisive, overwhelming. The allies were routed and sent flying in every direction. They had lost a large number of men and nearly all of their artillery. Napoleon, with originally inferior numbers, had not used all he had, had not thrown in his reserves. No wonder he addressed his troops in an exultant strain. "Soldiers, I am satisfied with you. In the battle of Austerlitz you have justified all my expectations by your intrepidity; you have adorned your eagles with immortal glory." No wonder that he told them that they were marked men, that on returning to France all they would need to say in order to command admiration would be: "I was at the battle of Austerlitz."

The results of this brief and brilliant campaign were various and striking. The Russians did not make peace, but withdrew in great disorder as best they could to their own country. But Austria immediately signed a peace and a very costly one, too. By the Treaty of Pressburg, dictated by Napoleon, who now had beaten her disastrously for the third time, she suffered her greatest humiliation, her severest losses. She ceded Venetia, a country she had held for eight years, since Campo Formio, to the Kingdom of Italy, whose king was Napoleon. Istria and Dalmatia also she ceded to Napoleon. Of all this coast-line of the upper Adriatic she retained only the single port of Trieste. Not Austria but France was henceforth the chief Adriatic power. The German principalities, Bavaria and Baden, had sided with Napoleon in the late campaign and Austria was now compelled to cede to each of them some of her valuable possessions in south Germany. Shut out of the Adriatic, shut out of Italy, Austria lost 3,000,000 subjects. She became nearly a land-locked country. Moreover she was compelled to acquiesce in other changes that Napoleon had made or was about to make in various countries.

Napoleon began now to play with zest the congenial role of Charlemagne about which he was prone to talk enthusiastically and with rhetorical extravagance. Having magically made himself Emperor, he now made others kings. As he abased mountains, so he exalted valleys. In the early months of 1806 he created four kings. He raised Bavaria and Württemberg, hitherto only duchies, to the rank of kingdoms, which they have since held, "in grateful recompense for the attachment they have shown the Emperor," he said. During the campaign the King of Naples had at a critical moment sided with his enemies. Napoleon therefore issued a simple decree, merely stating that the House of Bourbon had ceased to rule in Naples. He gave the vacant throne to his brother Joseph, two years older than himself. Joseph, who had first studied to become a priest, then to become an army officer, and still later to become a lawyer, now found himself a king, not by the grace of God, but by the grace of a younger brother.

The horn of plenty was not yet empty. Napoleon, after Austerlitz, forced the Batavian Republic, that is Holland, to become a monarchy and to accept his brother Louis, thirty-two years of age, as its king. Louis, as mild as his brother was hard, thought that the way to rule was to consult the interests and win the affections of his subjects. As this was not Napoleon's idea, Louis was destined to a rough and unhappy, and also brief, experience as king. "When men say of a king that he is a good man, it means that he is a failure," was the information that Napoleon sent Louis for his instruction.

The number of kingdoms at Napoleon's disposal was limited, temporarily at least. But he had many other favors to bestow, which were not to be despised. Nor were they despised. His sister Elise was made Princess of Lucca and Carrara, his sister Pauline, a beautiful and luxurious young creature, married Prince Borghese and became Duchess of Guastalla, and his youngest sister, Caroline, who resembled him in strength of character, married Murat, the dashing cavalry officer, who now became Duke of Berg, an artificial state which Napoleon created along the lower Rhine.

Two brothers, Lucien and Jerome, were not provided for, and thereby hangs a tale. Each had incurred Napoleon's displeasure, as each had married for love and without asking his consent. He had other plans for them and was enraged at their independence. Both were expelled from the charmed circle, until they should put away their wives and marry others according to Napoleon's taste, not theirs. This Lucien steadfastly refused to do, and so he, who by his presence of mind on the 19th Brumaire had saved the day and rendered all this story possible, stood outside the imperial favor, counting no more in the history of the times. When Jerome, the youngest member of this astonishing family, and made of more pliable stuff, awoke from love's young dream, and at the furious demands of Napoleon, put away his beautiful American bride, the Baltimore belle, Elizabeth Patterson, then he too became a king. All who worshiped Mammon in those exciting days received their appropriate reward.

It would be pleasant and very easy to continue this catalogue of favors, scattered right and left by the man who had rapidly grown so great. Officials of the state, generals of the army, and more distant relatives received glittering prizes and went on their way rejoicing, anxious for more. Appetite is said to grow by that on which it feeds.

More important far than this flowering of family fortunes was another result of the Austerlitz campaign, the transformation of Germany, effected by the French with the eager and selfish cooperation of many German princes. That transformation, which greatly reduced the distracting number of German states, by allowing some to absorb others, had already been going on for several years. When France acquired the German territory west of the river Rhine, it was agreed, in the treaties of Campo Formio and Luneville, that the princes thus dispossessed should receive compensations east of the river Rhine. This obviously could not be done literally and for all, as every inch of territory east of the Rhine already had its ruler. As a matter of fact the change was worked out by compensating only the hereditary rulers. There were, both on the left bank and on the right and all throughout Germany, many petty states whose rulers were not hereditary — ecclesiastical states, and free imperial cities. Now these were tossed to the princes who ruled by hereditary right, as compensation for the territories they had lost west of the river Rhine. This wholesale destruction of petty German states for the advantage of other lucky German states was accomplished not by the Germans themselves, which would have been shameless enough, but was accomplished in Paris. In the antechambers of the First Consul, particularly in the parlors of Talleyrand, the disgraceful begging for pelf went on. Talleyrand grew rapidly rich, so many were the "gifts" — one dreads to think what they would be called in a vulgar democracy — which German princes gave him for his support in despoiling their fellow Germans. For months the disgusting traffic went on, and when it ended in the "Conclusion" of March, 1803, really dictated by Bonaparte, the number of German principalities had greatly decreased. All the ecclesiastical states of Germany, with one single exception, had disappeared and of the fifty free cities only six remained. All went to enlarge other states. At least the map of Germany was simpler, but the position of the Church and of the Empire was greatly altered. Of the 360 states which composed the Holy Roman or German Empire in 1792 only eighty-two remained in 1805.

All this had occurred before Austerlitz. After Austerlitz the pace was increased, ending in the complete destruction of the Empire. Paris again became the center of German politics and intrigues, as in 1803. The result was that in 1806 the new kings of Bavaria and Württemberg and fourteen other German princes renounced their allegiance to the German Emperor, formed a new Confederation of the Rhine (July 12,

1806), recognized Napoleon as their "Protector," made an offensive and defensive alliance with him which gave to him the control of their foreign policy, the settlement of questions of peace and war, and guaranteed him 63,000 German troops for his wars. Fresh annexations to these states were made. Thus perished many more petty German states, eagerly absorbed by the fortunate sixteen.

Perished also the Holy Roman Empire which had been in existence, real or shadowy, for a thousand years. The secession of the sixteen princes and the formation of the Confederation of the Rhine killed it. It was only formal interment, therefore, when Napoleon demanded of the Emperor Francis, whom he had defeated at Austerlitz, that he renounce his title as Holy Roman Emperor. This Francis hastened to do (August 6, 1806), contenting himself henceforth with the new title he had given himself two years earlier, when Napoleon had assumed the imperial title. Henceforth he who had been Francis II of the Holy Roman Empire was called Francis I, Hereditary Emperor of Austria.

Napoleon, who could neither read nor speak a word of German, was now the real ruler of a large part of Germany, the strongest factor in German politics. To French domination of West Germany, annexed to France earlier, came an important increase of influence. It was now that French ideas began in a modified form to remold the civil life of South Germany. Tithes were abolished, the inequality of social classes in the eyes of the law was reduced though not destroyed, religious liberty was established, the position of the Jews was improved. The Germans lost in self-respect from this French domination, the patriotism of such as were patriotic was sorely wounded at the sight of this alien rule, but in the practical contrivances of a modernized social life, worked out by the French Revolution, and now in a measure introduced among them, they had a salutary compensation.

While all this shifting of scenes was being effected Napoleon had kept a large army in South Germany. The relations with Prussia, which country had been neutral for the past ten years, since the Treaty of Basel of 1795, were becoming strained and grew rapidly more so. The policy of the Prussian King, Frederick William III, was weak, vacillating, covetous. His diplomacy was playing fast and loose with his obligations as a neutral and with his desires for the territorial aggrandizement of Prussia. Napoleon's attitude was insolent and contemptuous. Both sides made an unenviable but characteristic record in double-dealing. The sordid details, highly discreditable to both, cannot be narrated here. Finally the war party in Berlin got the upper hand, led by the high-spirited and beautiful Queen Louise and by the military chiefs, relics of the glorious era of Frederick the Great, who thought they could do what Frederick had done, that is, defeat the French with ease. As if to give the world some intimation of the terrible significance of their displeasure they went to the French Embassy in Berlin and bravely whetted their swords upon its steps of stone. The royalist officers at Versailles in the early days of the Revolution had shown no more inane folly in playing with fire than did the Prussian military caste at this time. The one had learned its lesson. The other was now to go to the same pitiless school of experience.

Hating France and having an insensate confidence in their own superiority, the Prussian war party forced the government to issue an ultimatum to Napoleon, Emperor of the French, demanding that he withdraw his French troops beyond the Rhine. Napoleon knew better how to give ultimatums than how to receive them. He had watched the machinations of the Prussian ruling class with close attention. He was absolutely prepared when the rupture came. He now fell upon them like a cloudburst and administered a crushing blow in the two battles of Jena and Auerstadt, fought on the same day at those two places, a few miles apart (October 14, 1806), he himself in command of the former, Davout of the latter. The Prussians fought bravely, but their generalship was bad. Their whole army was disorganized, became panic-stricken, streamed from the field of battle as best it could, no longer receiving or obeying orders, many throwing away their arms, fleeing in every direction. Thousands of prisoners were taken and in succeeding days French officers scoured the country after the fugitives, taking thousands more. The collapse was complete. There was no longer any Prussian army. One after another all the fortresses fell.

On the 25th of October Napoleon entered Berlin in triumph. He had previously visited the tomb of Frederick the Great at Potsdam in order to show his admiration for his genius. He had the execrable taste, however, to take the dead Frederick's sword and sash and send them to Paris as trophies. "The entire kingdom of Prussia is in my hands," he announced. He planned that the punishment should be proportionate to his rage. He drew up a decree deposing the House of Hohenzollern but did not issue it, waiting for a more spectacular moment. He laid enormous war contributions upon the unhappy victim.

Napoleon postponed the announcement of the final doom until he should have finished with another enemy, Russia. Before leaving Berlin for the new campaign he issued the famous decrees which declared the British Isles in a state of blockade and prohibited commerce with them on the part of his dominions and those of his allies.

In the campaign of 1806 the Russians had been allied with the Prussians although they had taken no part, as the latter had not waited for them to come up. Napoleon now turned his attention to them. Going to Warsaw, the leading city of that part of Poland which Prussia had acquired in the partition of that country, he planned the new campaign, which was signalized by two chief battles, Eylau and Friedland. The former was one of the most bloody of his entire career. Fighting in the midst of a blinding snowstorm on February 8, 1807, Napoleon narrowly escaped defeat. The slaughter was frightful — "sheer butchery," said Napoleon later. "What carnage," said Ney, "and no results," thus accurately describing this encounter. Napoleon managed to keep the field and in his usual way he represented the battle as a victory. But it was a drawn battle. For the first time in Europe he had failed to win. The Russian soldiers fought with reckless bravery — "it was necessary to kill them twice," was the way the French soldiers expressed it.

Four months later, however, on June 14, 1807, on the anniversary of Marengo, Napoleon's star shone again unclouded. He won a victory at Friedland which, as he informed Josephine, "is the worthy sister of Marengo, Austerlitz, and Jena." The victory was at any rate so decisive that the Czar, Alexander I, consented to make overtures for peace. The Peace of Tilsit was concluded by the two Emperors in person after many interviews, the first one of which was held on a raft in the middle of the river Niemen. Not only did they make peace, but they went further and made a treaty of alliance, offensive and defensive. Napoleon gained a great diplomatic victory, which completely altered the previous diplomatic system of Europe, a fitting climax to three years of remarkable achievement upon the field of battle. Exercising upon Alexander all his powers of fascination, of flattery, of imagination, of quick and sympathetic understanding, he completely won him over. The two Emperors conversed in the most dulcet, rapturous way. "Why did not we two meet earlier?" exclaimed the enthusiastic Czar of All the Russia. With their two imperial heads bowed over a map of Europe they proceeded to divide it. Alexander was given to understand that he might take Finland, which he coveted, from Sweden, and attractive pickings from the vast Turkish Empire were dangled somewhat vaguely before him. On the other hand he recognized the changes Napoleon had made or was about to make in Western Europe, in Italy, and in Germany. Alexander was to offer himself as a mediator between those bitter enemies, England and France, and, in case England declined to make peace, then Russia would join France in enforcing the continental blockade, which was designed to bring England to terms.

Napoleon out of regard for his new friend and ally promised to allow Prussia still to exist. The decree dethroning the House of Hohenzollern was never issued. But Napoleon's terms to Prussia were very severe. She must give up all her territory west of the river Elbe. Out of this and other German territories Napoleon now made the Kingdom of Westphalia which he gave to his brother Jerome, who had by this time divorced his American wife. Prussia's eastern possessions were also diminished. Most of what she had acquired in the partitions of Poland was taken from her and created into the Grand Duchy of Warsaw, to be ruled over by the sovereign of Saxony, whose title of Elector Napoleon at this juncture now changed into that of King. These three states, Westphalia, Saxony, and the Duchy of Warsaw, now entered the Confederation of the Rhine, whose name thus became a misnomer, as the Confederation included not only the Rhenish and South German states but stretched from France to the Vistula, including practically all Germany except Prussia, now reduced to half her former size, and except Austria.

Naturally Napoleon was in high feather as he turned homeward. Naturally, also, he was pleased with the Czar. "He is a handsome good young emperor, with more mind than he is generally credited with" — such was Napoleon's encomium. Next to being sole master of all Europe came the sharing of mastery with only one other. A few months later he wrote his new ally that "the work of Tilsit will regulate the destinies of the world." There only remained the English, "the active islanders," not yet charmed or conquered. In the same letter to the Czar Napoleon refers to them as "the enemies of the world" and told how they could be easily brought to book. He had forgotten, or rather he had wished to have the world forget, that there was one monstrous flaw in the apparent perfection of his prodigious success. Two years before, on the very day after the capitulation of Ulm, Admiral Nelson had completely destroyed the French fleet in the battle of Trafalgar (October 21, 1805), giving his life that England might live and inspiring his own age and succeeding ages by the cry, "England expects every man to do his duty!"

The French papers did not mention the battle of Trafalgar, but it nevertheless bulks large in history. This was Napoleon's second taste of sea-power, his first having been, as we have seen, in Egypt, several years before, also at the hands of Nelson.

Napoleon returned to Paris in the pride of power and of supreme achievement. But, it is said, pride cometh before a fall. Was the race mistaken when it coined this cooling phrase of proverbial wisdom? It remained to be seen.

# CHAPTER IX

## THE EMPIRE AT ITS HEIGHT

AFTER Tilsit there remained England, always England, as the enemy of France. In 1805 Napoleon had defeated Austria, in 1806 Prussia, in 1807 Russia. Then the last-named power had shifted its policy completely, had changed partners, and, discarding its former allies, had become the ally of its former enemy.

Napoleon was now in a position to turn his attention to England. As she was mistress of the seas, as she had at the battle of Trafalgar in 1805 destroyed the French navy, the Emperor was compelled to find other means, if there were any, of humbling the elusive enemy. England must be beaten, but how? Napoleon now adopted a policy which the Convention and the Directory had originated. Only he gave to it a gigantic application and development. This was the Continental System, or the Continental Blockade. If England could not be conquered directly by French fleets and armies, she might be conquered indirectly.

England's power lay in her wealth, and her wealth came from her factories and her commerce which carried their products to the markets of the world, which brought her the necessary raw materials, and which kept open the fruitful connection with her scattered colonies. Cut this artery, prevent this commerce, close these markets, and her prosperity would be destroyed. Manufacturers would be compelled to shut down their factories. Their employees, thrown out of work, would face starvation. With that doom impending, the working classes and the industrial and commercial classes, threatened with ruin, would resort to terrific pressure upon the English government, to insurrections, if necessary, to compel it to sue for peace. Economic warfare was now to be tried on a colossal scale. By exhausting England's resources it was hoped and expected that England would be exhausted.

By the Berlin Decrees (November 1806) Napoleon declared a blockade of the British Isles, forbade all commerce with them, all correspondence, all trade in goods coming from England or her colonies, and ordered the confiscation and destruction of all English goods found in France or in any of the countries allied with her. No vessel coming from England or England's colonies should be admitted to their ports. To this England replied by severe Orders in Council, which Napoleon capped by additional decrees, issued from Milan.

This novel form of warfare had very important consequences. This struggle with England dominates the whole period from 1807 to 1814. It is the central thread that runs through all the tangled and tumultuous history of those years. There were plays within the play, complications and struggles with other nations which sometimes rose to such heights as momentarily to obscure the titanic contest between sea-power and land-power. But the fundamental, all-inclusive contest, to which all else was subsidiary or collateral, was the war to the knife between these two, England and France. Everywhere we see its influence, whether in Spain or Russia, in Rome or Copenhagen, along the Danube or along the Tagus.

The Continental System had this peculiarity, that, to be successful in annihilating English prosperity and power, it must be applied everywhere and constantly. The Continent must be sealed hermetically against English goods. Only then, with their necessary markets closed to them everywhere, would the English be forced to yield. Let there be a leak anywhere, let there be a strip of coast, as in Portugal or Spain or Italy, where English ships could touch and land their goods, and through that leak England could and would penetrate, could and would distribute her wares to eager customers, thus escaping the industrial strangulation intended by the Emperor of the French. This necessity Napoleon saw clearly. It was never absent from his mind. It inspired his conduct at every step. It involved him inevitably and, in the end, disastrously, in a policy of systematic and widespread aggressions upon other countries, consequently in a costly succession of wars.

To close simply the ports of France and of French possessions to English commerce would not at all accomplish the object aimed at. Napoleon must have the support of every other seaboard country in Europe. This he sought to get. He was willing to get it peacefully if he could, prepared to get it by violence, if he must. He secured the adhesion of Russia by the Treaty of Tilsit. Austria and Prussia, having been so decisively beaten, had to consent to apply the system to their dominions. Little Denmark, perforce, did the same when the demand came. Sweden, on the other hand, adhered to the English alliance. Consequently Russia was urged to take Finland, which belonged to Sweden, with its stretch of coast-line and its excellent harbors. Napoleon's brother Louis, King of Holland, would not enforce the blockade, as to do so meant the ruin of Holland. Consequently he was in the end forced to abdicate and Holland was annexed to France (1810). France also annexed the northern coasts of Germany up to Lübeck, including the fine ports of Bremen and Hamburg and the mouths of those rivers which led up into central Germany (1810). In Italy the Pope wished to remain neutral, but there must be no neutrals, in Napoleon's and also in England's opinion, if it could be prevented. In this case it could. Consequently Napoleon annexed part of the Papal States to the so-called Kingdom of Italy, of which he was himself the King, and part he incorporated directly and without ado into the French Empire (1809). Immediately the Pope excommunicated him and preached a holy war against the impious conqueror. Napoleon in turn took the Pope prisoner and kept him such for several years. This was injecting the religious element again into politics, as in the early days of the Revolution, to the profound embitterment of the times. Some of these events did not occur immediately after Tilsit, but did occur in the years from 1809 to 1811.

What did occur immediately after Tilsit was a famous and fatal misadventure in Portugal and Spain. Portugal stood in close economic and political relations with England and was reluctant to enforce the restrictions of the Continental Blockade. Her coast-line was too important to be allowed as an open gap. Therefore Napoleon arranged with Spain for the conquest and partition of that country. French and Spanish armies invaded Portugal, aiming at Lisbon. Before they arrived Napoleon had announced in his impressive and laconic fashion that "the fall of the House of Braganza furnishes one more proof that ruin is inevitable to whomsoever attaches himself to the English." The royal family escaped capture by sailing for the colony of Brazil and seeking safety beyond the ocean. There they remained until the overthrow of Napoleon. This joint expedition had given Napoleon the opportunity to introduce large bodies of troops into the country of his ally, Spain. They now remained there, under Murat, no one knew for what purpose. No one, except Napoleon, in whose mind a dark and devious plan was maturing. The French had dethroned the House of Bourbon in France during the Revolution. Napoleon had himself after Austerlitz dethroned the House of Bourbon in Naples and had put his brother Joseph in its place. There remained a branch of that House in Spain, and that branch was in a particularly corrupt and decadent state. The King, Charles IV, was utterly incompetent; the Queen grossly immoral and endowed with the tongue of a fishwife; her favorite and paramour, Godoy, was the real power behind the throne. The whole unsavory group was immensely unpopular in Spain. On the other hand, the King's son, Ferdinand, was idolized by the Spanish people, not because of anything admirable in his personality, which was utterly despicable, but because he was opposed to his father, his mother, and Godoy. Napoleon thought the situation favorable to his plan, which was to seize the throne thus occupied by a family rendered odious by its character and impotent by its dissensions. By a treacherous and hypocritical diplomacy he contrived to get Charles IV, the Queen, Godoy, and Ferdinand to come to Bayonne in southern France. No hungry spider ever viewed more coolly a more helpless prey entangled in his web. By a masterly use of the black arts of dissimulation, vituperation, and intimidation he swept the whole royal crew aside. Charles abdicated his throne into the hands of Napoleon, who thereupon forced Ferdinand to renounce his rights under a thinly veiled threat that, if he did not, the Duke d'Enghien would not be the only member of the House of Bourbon celebrated for an untoward fate. Ferdinand and his brothers were sent as prisoners to a chateau at

Valenay. The vacant throne was then given by Napoleon to his brother Joseph, who thereupon abdicated the kingship of Naples, which now passed to Murat, Napoleon's brother-in-law.

Napoleon later admitted that it was this Spanish business that destroyed him. "I embarked very badly on the Spanish affair, I confess; the immorality of it was too patent, the injustice too cynical." But this was the judgment of retrospect. He entered upon the venture with a light heart, confident that at most he would encounter only a feeble opposition. "Countries full of monks like yours," he told Ferdinand, "are easy to subdue. There may be some riots, but the Spaniards will quiet down when they see that I offer them the integrity of the boundaries of their kingdom, a liberal constitution, and the preservation of their religion and their national customs." Contrary to his expectation the conduct of the Spaniards was quite the reverse of this. He might offer them, as he did, better government than they had ever had. They hated him as a thief and trickster, also as a heretic, as a man whose character and policies and ideas were anathema. Napoleon embarked on a five years' war with them, which baffled him at every stage, drained his resources, in a contest that was inglorious, resources which should have been husbanded most carefully for more important purposes. "If it should cost me 80,000 men" to conquer Spain, "I would not attempt it," he said at the beginning, "but it will not take more than 12,000." A ghastly miscalculation, for it was to take 300,000 and to end in failure.

He encountered in Spain an opposition very different in kind and quality from any he had met hitherto in Italy or Germany, baffling, elusive, wearing. Previously he had waged war with governments only and their armies, not with peoples rising as one man, resolved to die rather than suffer the loss of their independence. The people of Italy, the people of Austria, the people of Germany, had not risen. Their governments had not appealed to them, but had relied upon their usual weapon, professional armies. Defeating these, as Napoleon had done with comparative ease, the governments had then sued for peace and endured his terms. No great wave of national feeling, daring all, risking all, had swept over the masses of those countries where he had hitherto appeared. France had herself undergone this very experience and her armies had won their great successes because they were aglow with the spirit of nationality, which had been so aroused and intensified by the Revolution. Now other countries were to take a page out of her book, at the very time that she was showing a tendency to forget that page herself. The Spanish rising was the first of a series of popular, national, instinctive movements that were to end in Napoleon's undoing.

The kind of warfare that the Spaniards carried on was peculiar, determined by the physical features of the land and by the circumstances in which they found themselves. Lacking the leadership of a government — their royal family being virtually imprisoned in France — poor and without large armies, they fought as guerrillas, little bands, not very formidable in themselves individually, but appearing now here, now there, now everywhere, picking off small detachments, stragglers, then disappearing into their mountain fastnesses. They thus repeated the history of their long struggles with the Moors. Every peasant had his gun and every peasant was inspired by loyalty to his country, and by religious zeal, as the Vendeans had been. The Catholic clergy entered again upon the scene, fanning the popular animosity against this despoiler of the Pope, and against these French free-thinkers. Napoleon had aroused two mighty forces which were to dog his footsteps henceforth, that of religious zeal, and that of the spirit of nationality, each with a fanaticism of its own.

Even geography, which Napoleon had hitherto made minister to his successes, was now against him. The country was poor, the roads were execrable, the mountains ran in the wrong direction, right across his path, the rivers also. In between these successive mountain ranges, in these passes and valleys, it was difficult for large armies, such as Napoleon's usually were, to operate. It was easy for mishaps to occur, for guerrilla bands or small armies to cut off lines of communication, for them to appear in front and in the rear at the same time. The country was admirable for the defensive, difficult for the offensive. This was shown early in the war when General Dupont was caught in a trap and obliged to capitulate with an army of 20,000 at Baylen (July 1808). This capitulation produced a tremendous impression throughout Europe. It was the first time a French army corps had been compelled to ground arms in full campaign. It was the heaviest blow Napoleon had yet received in his career. It encouraged the Spaniards, and other peoples also, who were only waiting to see the conqueror trip and who were now fired with hope that the thing might be done again. Napoleon was enraged, stormed against the unfortunate army, declared that from the beginning of the world nothing "so stupid, so silly, so cowardly" had been seen. They had had a chance to distinguish themselves, "they might have died," he said. Instead they had surrendered.

Joseph, the new king, who had been in his capital only a week, left it hurriedly and withdrew toward the Pyrenees, writing his brother that Spain was like no other country, that they must have an army of 50,000 to do the fighting, another of 50,000 to keep open the line of communications, and 100,000 gallows for traitors and scoundrels.

There was another feature of this war in the Peninsula, England's participation. An army was sent out under Sir Arthur Wellesley, later Duke of Wellington, to cooperate with the Portuguese and Spaniards. Wellesley, who had already distinguished himself in India, now began to build up a European reputation as a careful, original, and resourceful commander. Landing at Lisbon, the expedition shortly forced the French commander Junot to capitulate at Cintra (August 1808), as Dupont had been forced to in the preceding month at Baylen.

These were disasters which Napoleon could not allow to stand unanswered. His prestige, his reputation for invincibility must remain undiminished or Europe generally would become restless, with what result no one could foretell. He resolved therefore to go to Spain himself and show the Spaniards and all other peoples how hopeless it was to oppose him, how minor and casual defeats of his subordinates meant nothing, how his own mighty blows could no more be parried than before. But, before going, he wished to make quite sure of the general European situation. He arranged therefore for an interview at Erfurt in the center of Germany with his ally, Alexander of Russia. The two emperors spent a fortnight discussing their plans, examining every phase of the international situation (September-October 1808). This Erfurt Interview was the most spectacular episode in Napoleon's career as a diplomatist. He sought to dazzle Europe with his might, to impress the imaginations of men, and their fears, to show that the Franco-Russian alliance, concluded at Tilsit the year before, stood taut and firm and could not be shaken. All the kings and princes of Germany were summoned to give him, their "Protector," an appropriate and glittering setting. Napoleon brought with him the best theatrical troop in Europe, the company of the Theatre Franqais, and they played, as the pretentious expression was, to "a parterre of kings." On one occasion when Talma, the famous tragedian, recited the words,

> *"The friendship of a great man*
> *Is a true gift of the gods,"*

the Czar arose, seized Napoleon's hand, and gave the signal for applause. Day after day was filled with festivities, dinners, balls, hunts, reviews. The gods of German literature and learning, Goethe and Wieland, paid their respects. Meanwhile the two allies carefully canvassed the situation. In general the Czar was cordial, for he saw his profit in the alliance. But now and then a little rift in the lute appeared. One day, as they were discussing, Napoleon became angry, threw his hat on the floor and stamped upon it. Alexander merely observed, "You are angry, I am stubborn. With me anger gains nothing. Let's talk, let's reason together, or I shall leave."

The result of the interview was in the main satisfactory enough to both. The accord between the two seemed complete. The alliance was renewed, a new treaty was made, which was to be kept secret "for ten years at least," and now Napoleon felt free to direct his attention to the annoying Spanish problem, resolved to end it once for all. Assembling a splendid army of 200,000 men, he crossed the Pyrenees and in a brief campaign of a month he swept aside all obstacles with comparative ease, and entered Madrid (December 1808). There he remained a few weeks sketching the institutions of the new Spain which he intended to create. It would certainly have been a far more rational and enlightened and progressive state than it ever had been in the past. He declared the Inquisition, which still existed, abolished; also the remains of the feudal system; also the tariff boundaries which shut off province from province to the great detriment of commerce. He closed two-thirds of the monasteries, which were more than superabundant in this orthodox land. But, just as no individual cares to be reformed under the compulsion of a master, so the Spaniards would have nothing to do with these modern improvements in the social art, imposed by a heretic and a tyrant, who had wantonly filched their throne and invaded their country. Napoleon might perhaps have established his control over Spain so firmly that the new institutions might have struck root, despite this opposition. But time was necessary and time was something he could not command. In Madrid only a month, he was compelled to hurry back to France because of alarming news that reached him. He never returned to Spain.

Austria had thrown down the gauntlet again. It was entirely natural for her to seek at the convenient opportunity to avenge the humiliations she had repeatedly endured at the hands of France, to recover the position she had lost. Moreover the close alliance of Russia and France and Napoleon's seizure of the Spanish crown filled her with alarm. If Napoleon was capable of treating in this way a hitherto submissive ally, such as Spain had been, what might he not do to a chronic enemy and now a mere neutral like Austria, particularly as the latter had nowhere to look for support since Russia had deserted the cause. Moreover Austria had learned something from her disastrous experiences; among other things that her previous military system was defective in that it made no appeal to the people, to national sentiment. After Austerlitz the army was reorganized and a great militia was created composed of all men between the ages of eighteen and twenty-five. A promising invigoration of the national consciousness began. What occasion could be more convenient for paying off old scores and regaining lost ground than this, with Napoleon weakened by the necessity of holding down a spirited and outraged nation like the Spanish, resolved to go to any lengths, and by the necessity of checking or crushing the English in Portugal?

Under the influence of such considerations the war party gained the ascendency, and Austria, under the lead of Archduke Charles, brother of the Emperor and a very able commander, began a war in the spring of 1809. This war, which Napoleon did not seek, from which he had nothing to gain, was another Austrian mistake. Austria should have allowed more time for the full development of her new military system before running perilous risks again.

The Austrians paid for their precipitancy. Napoleon astonished them again by the rapidity of his movements. In April, 1809, he fought them in Bavaria, five battles in five days, throwing them back. Then he advanced down the Danube, entered Vienna without difficulty and crossed the river to the northern bank, whither the army of the Archduke had withdrawn. There Napoleon fought a two days' battle at Essling (May 21-22). The fighting was furious, the village of Essling changing hands nine times. Napoleon was seriously checked. He was obliged to take refuge for six weeks on the Island of Lobau in the Danube, until additional troops were brought up from Italy, and from Germany. Then, when his army was sufficiently reinforced, he crossed to the northern bank again and fought the great battle of Wagram (July 5-6). He was victorious, but in no superlative sense as at Austerlitz. The Archduke's army retired from the field in good order. The losses had been heavy, but no part of the army had been captured, none of the flags taken. This was the last victorious campaign fought by Napoleon. Even in it he had won his victory with unaccustomed difficulty. His army was of inferior quality, many of his best troops being detained by the inglorious Spanish adventure and the new soldiers proving inferior to the old veterans. Moreover he was encountering an opposition that was stronger in numbers, because of the army reforms just alluded to, while opposing generals were learning lessons from a study of his methods and were turning them against him. Archduke Charles, for instance, revered Napoleon's genius, but he now fought him tooth and nail and with ability.

After Wagram, Austria again made peace with Napoleon, the Peace of Vienna or of Schonbrunn. Austria was obliged to relinquish extensive territories. Galicia, which was the part of Poland she had acquired in the famous partitions, now went — a part of it to the Grand Duchy of Warsaw, a part of it to Russia. She was also forced to cede to France Trieste, Carniola, and part of Carinthia and Croatia. These were made into the Illyrian Provinces, which were declared imperial territory, although not formally annexed to

France. Austria lost 4,000,000 subjects, nearly a sixth of all that she possessed. She lost her only port and became entirely land-locked.

Having defeated Austria for the fourth time, Napoleon treated Europe to one of those swift transformation scenes of which he was fond as showing his easy and incalculable mastery of the situation. He contracted a marriage alliance with the House of Hapsburg which he had so repeatedly humbled, one of the proudest royal houses in Europe. He had long considered the advisability of a divorce from Josephine, as she had given him no heir and as the stability of the system he had erected depended upon his having one. At his demand the Senate dissolved his marriage with Josephine, and the ecclesiastical court in Paris was even more accomodating, declaring that owing to some irregularity the marriage had never taken place at all. Free thus by action of the State and the Church he asked the Emperor of Austria for the hand of his daughter, the Archduchess Marie Louise, and received it. This political marriage was considered advantageous on both sides. It seemed likely to prevent any further trouble between the two countries, to serve as a protection to Austria, to raise Napoleon's prestige by his connection with one of the oldest and proudest reigning houses of Europe, and to insure the continuance of the regime he had established with such display of genius. Thus only seventeen years after the execution of Marie Antoinette, another Austrian princess sat upon the throne of France. The marriage occurred in 1810 and in the following year was born the son for whom the title "King of Rome" stood ready.

# CHAPTER X

## THE DECLINE AND FALL OF NAPOLEON

NAPOLEON was now at the zenith of his power. He ruled directly over an empire that was far larger than the former Kingdom of France. In 1809 he annexed what remained of the Papal States in Italy, together with the incomparable city of Rome, thus ending, for the time at least, the temporal power of the Pope. In 1810 he forced his brother Louis to abdicate the kingship of Holland, which country was now incorporated in France. He also, as has been already stated, extended the empire along the northern coasts of Germany from Holland to Lübeck, thus controlling Hamburg, Bremen, and the mouths of the important German rivers. Each one of these annexations was in pursuance of his policy of the continental blockade, closing so much more of the coast-line of Europe to the commerce of England, the remaining enemy which he now expected to humble. He was Emperor of a state that had 130 departments. He was also King of Italy, a state in the north-eastern part of the peninsula. He was Protector of the Confederation of the Rhine, which included all Germany except Prussia and Austria, a confederation which had been enlarged since its formation by the addition of Westphalia and Saxony and the Grand Duchy of Warsaw, extending, therefore, clear up to Russia. His brother Joseph was King of Spain, his brother Jerome King of Westphalia, his brother-in-law Murat King of Naples. All were mere satellites of his, receiving and executing his orders. Russia was his willing ally. Prussia and Austria were his allies, the former because forced to be, the latter at first for the same reason, and later because she saw an advantage in it. No ruler in history had ever dominated so much of Europe. This supreme, incomparable pre-eminence had been won by his sword, supplemented by his remarkable statesmanship and diplomacy.

England alone remained outside the pale, England alone had not been brought to bend the knee to the great conqueror. Even she was breathing heavily, because the Continental System was inflicting terrible damage upon her. Factories were being forced to shut down, multitudes of laborers were being thrown out of work or were receiving starvation wages, riots and other evidences of unrest and even desperation seemed to indicate that even she must soon come to terms.

But this vast and imposing fabric of power rested upon uncertain bases. Built up, story upon story, by this highly imaginative and able mind, the architect left out of reckoning or despised the strains and stresses to which it was increasingly subjected. The rapidity with which this colossal structure fell to pieces in a few years shows how poorly consolidated it was, how rickety and precarious its foundations. Even a slight analysis will reveal numerous and foreboding elements of weakness beneath all this pomp and pageantry of power. Erected by the genius of a single man it depended solely upon his life and fortunes — and fortune is notoriously fickle. Built up by war, by conquest, it was necessarily environed by the hatred of the conquered. With every advance, every annexation, it annexed additional sources of discontent. Based on force, it could only be maintained by force. There could be and there was in all this vast extent of empire no common loyalty to the Emperor. Despotism, and Napoleon's regime was one of pitiless despotism, evoked no loyalty, only obedience based on fear. Europe has always refused to be dominated by a single nation or by a single ruler. It has run the risk several times in its history of passing under such a yoke, but it always in the end succeeded in escaping it. Universal dominion is an anachronism. The secret of Great Britain's hold upon many of the component parts of her empire lies in the fact that she allows them liberty to develop their own life in their own way. But such a conception was utterly beyond Napoleon, contrary to all his instincts and convictions. His empire meant the negation of liberty in the various countries which he dominated, France included. Napoleon's conquests necessarily ranged against him this powerful and unconquerable spirit. The more conquests, the more enemies, only waiting intently for the moment of liberation, scanning the horizon everywhere for the first sign of weakness which to them would be the harbinger of hope. This they found in Spain, and in the Austrian campaign of 1809 in which the machinery of military conquest had creaked, had worked clumsily, had threatened at one moment to break down.

There was a force in the world which ran directly counter to Napoleon's projects, the principle of nationality. Napoleon despised this feeling, and in the end it was his undoing. He might have seen that it had been the strength of France a few years earlier, that now this spirit had passed beyond the natural boundaries and was waking into a new life, was nerving to a new vigor, countries like Spain, even Austria and, most conspicuously, Prussia.

Prussia after Jena underwent the most serious humiliation a nation can be called to endure. For several years she was under the iron heel of Napoleon, who kept large armies quartered on her soil, who drained her resources, who interfered peremptorily in the management of her government, who forbade her to have more than 42,000 soldiers in her army. But out of the very depths of this national degradation came Prussia's salvation. Her noblest spirits were aroused to seek the causes of this unexpected and immeasurable national calamity and to try to remedy them. From 1808 to 1812 Prussians, under the very scrutiny of Napoleon, who had eyes but did not see, worked passionately upon the problem of national regeneration. The result surpassed belief. A tremendous national patriotism was aroused by the poets and thinkers, the philosophers and teachers, all bending their energies to the task of quickening among the youth the spirit of unselfish devotion to the fatherland. An electric current of enthusiasm, of idealism, swept through the educational centers and through large masses of the people. The University of Berlin, founded in 1809, in Prussia's darkest hour, was, from the beginning, a dynamic force. It and other universities became nurseries of patriotism.

Prussia underwent regeneration in other ways. Particularly memorable was the work of two statesmen, Stein and Hardenberg. Stein, in considering the causes of Prussia's unexampled woes, came to the conclusion that they lay in her defective or harmful social and legal institutions. The masses of Prussia were serfs, bound to the soil, their personal liberty gravely restricted, and, as Stein said, "patriots cannot be made out of serfs." He persuaded the King to issue an edict of emancipation, abolishing serfdom. The Prussian king, he said, was no longer "the king of slaves, but of free men." Many other reforms were passed abolishing or reducing class distinctions and privileges. In all this Stein was largely imitating the French Revolutionists who by their epoch-making reforms had released the energies of the French so that their power had been vastly multiplied. The army, too, was reorganized, opportunity was opened to talent, as in France, with what magical results we have seen. As Napoleon forbade that the Prussian army should number more than 42,000 men, the ingenious device was hit upon of having men serve with the colors only a brief time, long enough to learn the essentials of the soldier's life. Then they would pass into the reserve and others would be put rapidly through the same training. By this method several times 42,000 men received a military training whose effectiveness was later to be proved.

Thus Prussia's regeneration went on. The new national spirit, wonderfully invigorated, waited with impatience for its hour of probation. It should be noted, however, that these reforms, which resembled in many respects those accomplished in France by the Constituent Assembly and the Convention, and which were in fact suggested by them, rested, however, on very different principles. There was in Prussia no assertion of the Rights of Man, no proclamation of the people as sovereign. In Prussia it was the king who made the reforms, not the people. The theory of the divine right of the monarch was not touched, but was maintained as sacred as ever. There was reform in Prussia but no revolution. Prussia took no step toward democracy. This distinction has colored the whole subsequent history of that kingdom and colors it today. "Everything for the people, nothing by the people," was evidently the underlying principle in this work of national reorganization. Even these reforms were not carried out completely, owing to opposition from within the kingdom and from without. But, though incomplete, they were very vitalizing.

Napoleon's policies had created other enmities in abundance which were mining the ground beneath him. His treatment of the Pope, whom he held as a prisoner and whose temporal power he had abolished by incorporating his states, a part in the French Empire and a part in the Kingdom of Italy, made the Catholic clergy everywhere hostile, and offended the faithful. Rome, hitherto the papal capital, was declared the second city of the Empire and served as a title for Napoleon's son. All rights of the Pope were thus cavalierly ignored. The subtle and vast influence of the church was of course now directed to the debasement of the man it had previously conspicuously favored and praised. In addition to combating the rising tide of nationality, Napoleon henceforth also had his quarrel with the Papacy.

Into these entanglements he had been brought by the necessities of his conflict with England, by the continental blockade. For it was that system that drove him on from one aggression to another, from annexation to annexation. That system, too, created profound discontent in all the countries of the continent, including France itself. By enormously raising the price of such necessaries as cotton and sugar and coffee and tea, products of Britain's colonies or of the tropical countries with which she traded, they introduced hardship and irritation into every home. The normal course of business was turned inside out and men suddenly found their livelihood gone and ruin threatening or already upon them. To get the commodities to which they were accustomed they smuggled on a large and desperate scale. This led to new and severe regulations and harsher punishments, and thus the tyrannical interference in their private lives made multitudes in every country hate the tyranny and long for its overthrow. Widespread economic suffering was the inevitable result of the continental system and did more to make Napoleon's rule unpopular throughout Europe than did anything else except the enormous waste of life occasioned by the incessant warfare. That system, too, was the chief cause of the rupture of the alliance between Russia and France, in 1812, a rupture which led to appalling disaster for Napoleon and was the beginning of the end. The whole stupendous superstructure of Napoleonic statecraft and diplomacy fell like a house of cards in the three years 1812, 1813, and 1814.

The Franco-Russian alliance, concluded so hastily and unexpectedly at Tilsit in 1807, lasted nominally nearly five years. It was, however, unpopular from the beginning with certain influential classes in Russia and its inconveniences became increasingly apparent. The aristocracy of Russia, a powerful body, hated this alliance with a country which had abolished its own nobility, leaving its members impoverished by the loss of their lands and privileges. There could be no sympathy between the Russian nobility, based upon the grinding serfdom of the masses, and the country which had swept all traces of feudalism aside and proclaimed the equality of men. Moreover the Russian nobility hated the continental system, as it nearly destroyed the commerce with England in wheat, flax, and timber, which was the chief source of their wealth. Furthermore, the Czar Alexander I, having obtained some of the advantages he had expected from his alliance, was irritated, now that he did not obtain others for which he had hoped. He had gained Finland from Sweden and the Danubian Principalities from Turkey, but the vague though alluring prospect of a division of the Turkish Empire still remained unfulfilled and was, indeed, receding into the limbo of the unlikely. He wanted Constantinople, and Napoleon made it clear he could never have it. Moreover Alexander was alarmed by Napoleon's schemes with the Grand Duchy of Warsaw, a state made out of the Polish provinces which had been acquired by Prussia and Austria. Alexander had no objection to Prussia and Austria losing their Polish provinces, but he himself had Polish provinces and he dreaded anything that looked like a resurrection of the former Kingdom of Poland, any appeal to the Polish national feeling.

But the main cause of Alexander's gradual alienation from his ally was the continental blockade. This was working great financial loss to Russia. Moreover its inconveniences were coming home to him in other ways. To enforce the system more completely in Germany Napoleon seized in 1811 the Grand Duchy of Oldenburg, which belonged to Alexander's brother-in-law.

Thus the alliance was being subjected to a strain it could not stand. In 1812 it snapped, and loud was the report. Napoleon would not allow any breach of the continental blockade if he could prevent it. He resolved to force Russia, as he had forced the rest of the continent, to do his bidding. He demanded that she live up to her promises and exclude British commerce. The answers were evasive, unsatisfactory, and in June, 1812, Napoleon crossed the Niemen with the largest army he ever commanded, over half a million men, the "army of twenty nations," as the Russians called it. About one-half were French. The rest were a motley host of Italians, Danes, Croatians, Dalmatians, Poles, Dutchmen, Westphalians, Saxons, Bavarians, Württembergers, and still others. For the first time in his military career Napoleon commanded the cooperation of Austria and Prussia, both of which were compelled to send contingents. There were 100,000 cavalry and a numerous and powerful artillery. He had around him a brilliant staff of officers, Murat, Ney, Eugene Beauharnais, and others. It seemed as if no power on earth could resist such an engine of destruction. Napoleon himself spoke of the expedition as the "last act" of the play.

It was not quite that, but it was a supremely important act, one full of surprises. From the very start it was seen that in numbers there is sometimes weakness, not strength. This vast machine speedily commenced to give way beneath its own weight. The army had not advanced five days before the commissary department began to break down and bread was lacking. Horses, improperly nourished, died by the thousands, thus still further demoralizing the commissariat and imperiling the artillery. The Russians adopted the policy of not fighting but constantly retreating, luring the enemy farther and farther into a country which they took the pains to devastate as they retired, leaving no provisions or supplies for the invaders, no stations for the incapacitated, as they burned their villages on leaving them. Napoleon seeking above everything a battle, in which he hoped to crush the enemy, was denied the opportunity. The Russians had studied the Duke of Wellington's methods in Portugal and profited by their study. It was 700 miles from the Niemen to Moscow. Napoleon had had no intention of going so far, but the tactics of his enemy forced him steadily to proceed. The Czar had announced that he would retire into Asia if necessary, rather than sign a peace with his enemy on the sacred soil of Russia. Napoleon hoped for a battle at Smolensk, but only succeeded in getting a rear-guard action and a city in flames.

This policy of continual retreat, so irritating to the French Emperor, was equally irritating to the Russian people, who did not understand the reason and who clamored for a change. The Russians therefore took up a strong position at Borodino on the route to Moscow. There a battle occurred on September 7, 1812, between the French army of 125,000 men and the Russian of 100,000. The battle was one of the bloodiest of the whole epoch. The French lost 30,000, the Russians 40,000 men. Napoleon's victory was not overwhelming, probably because he could not bring himself to throw in the Old Guard. The Russians retreated in good order, leaving the road open to Moscow, which city Napoleon entered September 14. The army had experienced terrible hardships all the way, first over roads soaked by constant rains, then later over roads intensely heated by July suns and giving forth suffocating clouds of dust. Terrible losses, thousands a day, had characterized the march of 700 miles from the Niemen to Moscow.

Napoleon had resolved on the march to Moscow expecting that the Russians would consent to peace, once the ancient capital was in danger. But no one appeared for that purpose. He found Moscow practically deserted, only 15,000 there, out of a population of 250,000. Moreover the day after his entry fires broke out in various parts of the city, probably set by Russians. For four days the fearful conflagration raged, consuming a large part of the city. Still Napoleon stayed on, week after week, fearing the effect that the news of a retreat might produce, and hoping, against hope, that the Czar would sue for peace. Finally there was nothing to do, after wasting a month of precious time, but to order the retreat. This was a long-drawn-out agony, during which an army of 100,000 men was reduced to a few paltry thousands, fretted all along the route by which they had come by Russian armies and by Cossack guerrilla bands, horrified by the sight of thousands of their comrades still unburied on the battlefield of Borodino, suffering indescribable hardships of hunger and exhaustion and finally caught in all the horrors of a fierce Russian winter, clad, as many of them were, lightly for a summer campaign. The scenes that accompanied this flight and rout were of unutterable woe, culminating in the hideous tragedy of the crossing of the Beresina, the bridge breaking down under the wild confusion of men fighting to get across, horses frightened, the way blocked by carts and wagons, the bridges raked by the fire of the Russian artillery. Thousands were left behind, many fell or threw themselves into the icy river and were frozen to death. In the river, says one writer, when the Russians came up later they saw "awful heaps of drowned soldiers, women, and children, emerging above the surface of the waters, and here and there rigid in death like statues on their ice-bound horses." A few thousand out of all the army finally got out of Russia and across the Niemen. Many could only crawl to the hospitals asking for "the rooms where people die." History has few ghastlier pages in all its annals. Napoleon himself left the army on December 5th, and traveled rapidly incognito to Paris, which he reached on the 18th. "I shall be back on the Niemen in the spring," was the statement with which he tried to make men think that the lost position would be soon recovered.

He did not quite keep the promise. He did not get as far back again as the Niemen. But 1813 saw him battling for his supremacy in Germany, as 1812 had seen him battling for it in Russia. The Russian disaster had sent a thrill of hope through the ranks of his enemies everywhere. The colossus might be, indeed appeared to be, falling. Had not the auspicious moment arrived for annihilating him? Particularly violent was the hatred of the Prussians, who had, more than other peoples, felt the ruthlessness of his tyranny for the last six years. They trembled with eagerness to be let loose and when their King made a treaty of alliance with Russia and subsequently made a more direct and personal appeal to his people than any Prussian monarch had ever made before, they responded enthusiastically. There was a significant feature about this Treaty of Kalisch with Russia. Russia was not to lay down her arms against Napoleon until Prussia had recovered an area equal to that which she had possessed before the battle of Jena. But the area was not to be the same, for Russia was to keep Prussia's Polish provinces, now included in the Grand Duchy of Warsaw, whose doom was decreed. Prussia should have compensation in northern Germany.

Could Napoleon rely on the Confederation of the Rhine and on his ally Austria? This remained to be seen. A reverse would almost surely cost him the support of the former and the neutrality of the latter. Their loyalty would be proportioned to his success. There was with them not the same popular wrath as with the Prussians. On the other hand, their princes had a keen eye for the main chance. Austria surely would use Napoleon's necessities for her own advantage. The princes of the Rhenish Confederation wished to retain the advantages they had won largely through their complaisant cooperation with Napoleon during recent years. Austria wished to recover advantages she had lost, territory, prestige, badly tattered and torn by four unsuccessful campaigns.

Napoleon, working feverishly since the return from Russia, finally got an army of over 200,000 men together. But to do this he had to draw upon the youth of France, as never before, calling out recruits a year before their time for service was due. A large part of them were untrained, and had to get their training on the march into Germany. The army was weak in cavalry, a decisive instrument in following up a victory and clinching it.

Napoleon was back in central Germany before the Russians and Prussians were fully prepared. He defeated them at Lutzen and at Bautzen in May, 1813, but was unable to follow up his victories because of the lack of sufficient cavalry, and the campaign convinced him that he could accomplish nothing decisive without reinforcements. He therefore agreed, in an unlucky moment, as it later proved, to a six weeks' armistice. During that time he did get large reinforcements but his enemies got larger. And during that interval the diplomatic intriguing went against him so that when the armistice was over Austria had joined the alliance of Russia, Prussia, and England, against him. He defeated the Austrians at Dresden (August 26-27), his last great victory. His subordinates were, however, beaten in subsidiary engagements and he was driven back upon Leipsic. There occurred a decisive three days' battle, the "Battle of the Nations," as the Germans call it (October 16-18). In point of numbers involved this was the greatest battle of the Napoleonic era. Over half a million men took part, at most 200,000 under Napoleon, 300,000 under the commanders of the allies. Napoleon was disastrously defeated and was sent flying back across the Rhine with only a small remnant of his army. The whole political structure which he had built up in Germany collapsed. The members of the Confederation of the Rhine deserted the falling star, and entered the alliance against him, on the guarantee of their possessions by the allies. Jerome fled from Westphalia and his brief kingdom disappeared. Meanwhile Wellington, who for years had been aiding the Spaniards, had been successful and was crossing the Pyrenees into southern France. The coils were closing in upon the lion, who now stood at bay.

The allies moved on after the retreating French toward the Rhine. It had been no part of their original purpose to demand Napoleon's abdication. They now, in November 1813, offered him peace on the basis of the natural frontiers of France, the Rhine, the Alps, and the Pyrenees. He would not accept but procrastinated, and made counter-propositions. Even in February 1814 he could have retained his throne and the historic boundaries of the old Bourbon monarchy, had he been willing to renounce the rest. He dallied with the suggestion, secretly hoping for some turn in luck that would spring the coalition apart and enable him to recover the ground he had lost. In thus refusing to recognize defeat, refusing to accept an altered situation, he did great harm to France and completed his own downfall. His stiff, uncompromising, unyielding temper sealed his doom. He was no longer acting as the wise statesman, responsible for the welfare of a great people who, by their unstinted sacrifices, had put him under heavy obligations. His was the spirit of the gambler, thinking to win all by a happy turn of the cards. He was also will incarnate. With will and luck all might yet be retrieved.

He had said, on leaving Germany, "I shall be back in May with 250,000 men." He did not expect a winter campaign and he felt confident that by May he could have another army. The allies, however, did not wait for May, but at the close of December 1813 streamed across the Rhine and invaded France from various directions. France, victorious for eighteen years, now experienced what she had so often administered to others. The campaign was brief, only two months, February and March 1814. Napoleon was hopelessly outnumbered. Yet this has been called the most brilliant of his campaigns. Fighting on the defensive and on inner lines, he showed marvelous mastery of the art of war, striking here, striking there with great precision and swiftness, undaunted, resourceful, tireless. The allies needed every bit of their overwhelming superiority in numbers to compass the end of their redoubtable antagonist, with his back against the wall and his brain working with matchless lucidity and with lightning-like rapidity. They thought they could get to his capital in a week. It took them two months. However, there could be but one end to such a campaign, if the allies held together, as they did. On the 30th of March Paris capitulated and on the following day the Czar Alexander and Frederick William III, the King of Prussia, made their formal entry into the city which the Duke of Brunswick twenty-two years before had threatened with destruction if it laid sacrilegious hands upon the King or Queen. Since that day much water had flowed under the bridge, and France and Europe had had a strange history, signifying much.

The victors would no longer tolerate Napoleon. He was forced to abdicate unconditionally. He was allowed to retain his title of Emperor, but henceforth he was to rule only over Elba, an island nineteen miles long and six miles wide, lying off the coast of Tuscany, whence his Italian ancestors had sailed for Corsica two centuries and a half before he was born. Thither he repaired, having said farewell to the Old Guard in the courtyard of the palace of Fontainebleau, kissing the flag of France made lustrous on a hundred fields. "Nothing but sobbing was heard in all the ranks," wrote one of the soldiers who saw the scene, "and I can say that I too shed tears when I saw my Emperor depart."

On the day that Napoleon abdicated, the Senate, so-called guardian of the constitution, obsequious and servile to the Emperor in his days of fortune, turned to salute the rising sun, and in solemn session proclaimed Louis XVIII King of France. The allies, who had conquered Napoleon and banished him to a petty island in the Mediterranean, thought they were done with him for good and all. But from this complacent self-assurance they were destined to a rude awakening. Their own errors and wranglings at the Congress of Vienna, whither they repaired in September 1814 to divide the spoils and determine the future organization of Europe, and the mistakes and indiscretions of the Bourbons whom they restored to rule in France, gave Napoleon the opportunity for the most audacious and wonderful adventure of his life.

Louis XVIII, the new king, tried to adapt himself to the greatly altered circumstances of the country to which he now returned in the wake of foreign armies after an absence of twenty-two years. He saw that he could not be an absolute king as his ancestors had been, and he therefore granted a Charter to the French, giving them a legislature and guaranteeing certain rights which they had won and which he saw could not safely be withdrawn. His regime assured much larger liberty than France had ever experienced under Napoleon. Nevertheless certain attitudes of his and ways of speaking, and the actions of the royalists who surrounded him, and several unwise measures of government, soon rendered him unpopular and irritated and alarmed the people. He spoke of himself as King by the grace of God, thus denying the sovereignty of the people; he dated his first document, the Charter, from "the nineteenth year of my reign," as if there had never been a Republic and a Napoleonic Empire; he restored the white flag and banished the glorious tricolor which had been carried in triumph throughout Europe. What was much more serious, he offended thousands of Napoleon's army officers by retiring or putting them on half-pay, many thus being reduced to destitution, and all feeling themselves dishonored. Moreover many former nobles who had early in the Revolution emigrated from France and then fought against her received honors and distinctions. Then, in addition, the Roman Catholic clergy and the nobles of the court talked loudly and unwisely about getting back their lands which had been confiscated and sold to the peasants, although both the Concordat of 1802 and the Charter of 1814 distinctly recognized and ratified these changes and promised that they should not be disturbed. The peasants were far and away the most numerous class in France, and they were thus early alienated from the Bourbons by these threats at their most vital interest, their property rights, which Napoleon had always stoutly maintained. Thus a few months after Napoleon's abdication the evils of his reign were forgotten, the terrible cost in human life, the burdensome taxation, the tyranny of it all, and he was looked upon as a friend, as a hero to whom the soldiers had owed glory and repute and the peasants the secure possession of their farms. In this way a mental atmosphere hostile to Louis XVIII, and favorable to Napoleon, was created by a few months of Bourbon rule.

Napoleon, penned up in his little island, took note of all this. He also heard of the serious dissensions of the allies now that they were trying to divide the spoils at Vienna, of their jealousies and animosities, which, in January 1815, rose to such a pitch that Austria, France, and England prepared to go to war with Prussia and Russia over the allotment of the booty. He also knew that they were intriguing at the Congress for his banishment to some place remote from Europe.

For ten months he had been in his miniature kingdom. The psychological moment had come for the most dramatic action of his life. Leaving the island with twelve hundred guards, and escaping the vigilance of the British cruisers, he landed at Cannes on March 1. That night he started on the march to Paris and on March 20 entered the Tuileries, ruler of France once more. The return from Elba will always remain one of the most romantic episodes of history. With a force so small that it could easily have been taken prisoner, he had no alternative and no other wish than to appeal directly to the confidence of the people. Never was there such a magnificent response. All along the route the peasants received him enthusiastically. But his appeal was particularly to the army, to whom he issued one of his stirring bulletins. "Soldiers," it began, "we have not been conquered. We were betrayed. Soldiers! Come and range yourselves under the banner of your chief: his existence depends wholly on yours: his interests, his honor, and his glory are your interests, your honor, your glory. Come! Victory will march at double-quick. The eagle with the national colors shall fly from steeple to steeple to the towers of Notre Dame. Then you will be able to show your scars with honor: then you will be able to boast of what you have done: you will be the liberators of your country."

Regiment after regiment went over to him. The royalists thought he would be arrested at Grenoble, where there was a detachment of the army under a royalist commander. Napoleon went straight up to them, threw open his grey coat, and said, "Here I am: you know me. If there is a soldier among you who wishes to shoot his Emperor, he can do it." The soldiers flocked over to him, tearing off the white cockades and putting on the tricolor, which they had secretly carried in their knapsacks. Opposition melted away all along the route. It became a triumphant procession. When lies would help Napoleon told them — among others that it was not ambition that brought him back, that "the forty-five best heads of the government of Paris have called me from Elba and my return is supported by the three first powers of Europe." He admitted that he had made mistakes and assured the people that henceforth he desired only to follow the paths of peace and liberty. He had come back to protect the threatened blessings of the Revolution. The last part of this intoxicating journey he made in a carriage attended by only a half-dozen Polish lancers. On March 20 Louis XVIII fled from the Tuileries. That evening Napoleon entered it.

"What was the happiest period of your life as Emperor?" someone asked him at St. Helena. "The march from Cannes to Paris," he instantly replied.

His happiness was limited to less than the "Hundred Days" which this period of his reign is called. Attempting to reassure France and Europe, he met from the former, tired of war, only half-hearted support, from the allies only remorseless opposition. When the diplomats at the Congress of Vienna heard of his escape from Elba they immediately ceased their contentions and banded themselves together against "this disturber of the peace of Europe." They declared him an outlaw and set their armies in motion. He saw that he must fight to maintain himself. He resolved to attack before his enemies had time to effect their union. The battlefield was in Belgium, as Wellington with an army of English, Dutch, Belgians, and Germans, and, at some distance from them, Blucher with a large army of Prussians, were there. If Napoleon could prevent their union, then by defeating each separately, he would be in a stronger position when the Russian and Austrian armies came on. Perhaps, indeed, they would think it wiser not to come on at all but to conclude peace. In Belgium consequently occurred a four days' campaign culminating on the famous field of Waterloo, twelve miles south of Brussels. There on a hot Sunday in June Napoleon was disastrously defeated (June 18, 1815). The sun of Austerlitz set forever. The battle, begun at half-past eleven in the morning, was characterized by prodigies of valor, by tremendous charges of cavalry and infantry back and forth over a sodden field. Wellington held his position hour after hour as wave after wave of French troops rushed up the hill, foaming in and about the solid unflinching British squares, then, unable to break them, foamed back again. Wellington held on, hoping, looking for the Prussians under Blucher, who, at the beginning of the battle, were eleven miles away. They had promised to join him, if he accepted battle there, and late in the afternoon they kept the promise. Their arrival was decisive, as Napoleon was now greatly outnumbered. In the early evening, as the sun was setting, the last charge of the French was repulsed. Repulse soon turned into a rout and the demoralized army streamed from the field in utter panic, fiercely pursued by the Prussians. The Emperor, seeing the utter annihilation of his army, sought death, but sought in vain. "I ought to have died at Waterloo," he said later, "but the misfortune is that when a man seeks death most he cannot find it. Men were killed around me, before, behind — everywhere. But there was no bullet for me." He fled to Paris, then toward the western coast of France hoping to escape to the United States, but the English cruisers off the shore rendered that impossible. Making the best of necessity he threw himself upon the generosity of the British. "I have come," he announced, "like Themistocles, to seek the hospitality of the British nation." Instead of receiving it, however, he was sent to a rock in the South Atlantic, the island of St. Helena, where he was kept under a petty and ignoble surveillance. Six years later he died of cancer of the stomach at the age of fifty-two, leaving an extraordinary legend behind him to disturb the future. He was buried under a slab that bore neither name nor date, and it was twenty years before he was borne to his final resting-place under the dome of the Invalides in Paris, although in his last will and testament he said: "My wish is to be buried on the banks of the Seine in the midst of the French people whom I have loved so well."